SIMPLE AND SUCCESSFUL INVESTING

I DID IT, AND YOU CAN TOO!

By: Brian Borgford

Copyright © 2015 Brian Borgford

All rights reserved.

ISBN: 1517653118
ISBN-13: 978-1517653118

Acknowledgements

I would like to thank the following people who provided helpful reviews and comments of the initial drafts of this book.

David Progosh

John Mather

Patreshia Tkach

Beth Gerstenberger

Alistair Vogan

Patrick Berting

Contents

PREFACE AND PRELUDE 1
INTRODUCTION 5
CHAPTER 1 - DEFINITION OF INVESTING 9
CHAPTER 2 - MY RESULTS 11
CHAPTER 3 - MY STRATEGY 19
CHAPTER 4 - EVOLUTION OF MY INVESTMENT STRATEGY 23
CHAPTER 5 - SUGGESTED STOCKS 29
CHAPTER 6 - DIY - HOW CAN I DO IT MYSELF? 35
CHAPTER 7 - MARKETS, TERMINOLOGY AND INVESTMENT INSTRUMENTS 41
CHAPTER 8 - GO INTERNATIONAL 53
CHAPTER 9 - TYPES OF INVESTORS AND STRATEGIES 57
CHAPTER 10 - CALCULATING RETURNS 65
CHAPTER 11 - FINANCIAL ADVISORS 79
CHAPTER 12 - REAL ESTATE 85
CHAPTER 13 - MARKET HISTORY 109
CHAPTER 14 - FLUBS AND PRIZES 115
CHAPTER 15 - MY HISTORY 125
CHAPTER 16 - NOW TO TODAY 141
SUMMARY AND CONCLUSION 143

Preface and Prelude

Who should read this book?

This book is written for those individuals who want to manage their own finances and who have some money to invest or expect to have some money to invest. It could be as little as $10,000 but to take full advantage of the information contained herein, you should likely have at least in the neighbourhood of $100,000. And you may have money you didn't even know about.

One of the best places to find money that you didn't know you had is in your pension fund. If your pension sits with a current employer, let it sit there as you likely don't have much flexibility on what to do with it. If, however, you have changed employers, as many of us have done, you probably have an accumulation of investable wealth that you didn't know you had. Open a self-directed RRSP (Canada) or a similar investment account with your IRA (U.S.) and move your funds into it and begin taking control of your financial future. That is how I started.

About this book

This is not a highly polished piece of literature, but rather, a simple representation of my thoughts and experience on investing*. Occasionally you may see duplication of information as you read. This is intentional as I think you need to see an idea in several contexts. However, if you see spelling and grammatical errors, feel free to let me know and I will try to make corrections in subsequent editions.

I have attempted to present the information with a logical flow with the more relevant information at the front and the background information towards the end, but don't be surprised if it reads like a series of discrete essays. Many of the sections are just that, essays that I have previously presented in my blog.

https://borgfordinvesting.wordpress.com/

I try to present everything in this book using fact and evidence, not hypothetical scenarios or biased feelings. Feel free to criticize my approach, but it is difficult to criticize the results; not many people have done better. As a matter of fact I am still looking for the individual who has provable results that are actually better than mine. I know there are fund managers who will claim better results, but again show me an individual's actual personal portfolio performance that is better than mine. I always say, "Show Me". It is easy to run some numbers to tell a story, but if you think you can do better, "Show Me" your results, don't just tell me how you would do it or how it could be done.

I will start out with my results and returns and gradually dig deeper into the background behind them and the various strategies used. I try not to dwell on complicated investment terminology. Many advisors will try to WOW you with their language but language doesn't produce results. I will try to explain any terms that I use. If there is anything you don't understand, feel free to ask me - either through my email address provided, or through comments on my website.

I hope you will find this book of some value for your financial planning purposes.

Brian Borgford

brianborgford@hotmail.com

* Please see any of the several other books of a more literary nature that I've written at:

http://www.amazon.com/Brian-Borgford/e/B0088L0ULC

Introduction

Why should you read this book? What makes it any different than any other book about investing?

In answer to the first question - **results**. I have a track record that most investment advisors would envy, but never admit to that envy. The process I have used to achieve these results is not complex or difficult to understand. It can be done by any ordinary wage earner - because that is what I am (or was until I retired). I am not a one hit wonder who had a good year or two. I have many years of sustained results.

I spent twenty years trying all the get rich quick schemes I could find and achieved dismal results. With a change of strategy, I had ten years of mediocre to good results. Once I finally hit on my current strategy there has been no looking back. From about the year 2000 to date, my results have been excellent. That includes "The Lost Decade" for investing from 2000 to 2010 which also included the biggest market crash since "The Great Depression." I not only survived, I thrived.

What makes this book different? I am not a self-proclaimed financial guru who is telling you what you should do. Most books on investing are just that. These gurus never disclose their financial status or their own track record. This is not a "how to" book with a lot of "you shoulds" in it, although I do provide some steps to follow should you decide it is for you. The book is about my background and experience and how I got where I am. You can choose to follow it yourself, or just read it for enjoyment. I'm not trying to convert anyone, just share my experience.

What are my results? At the time of publication, I am 63 years old and in retirement without a company pension. I am not a member of the ultra-rich crowd, but I have become reasonably self-sufficient. A bit of research will show you that only about one percent of the population has over a million dollars in investable assets - also referred to as high-net-worth individuals. I qualify as a high-net-worth individual, having entered that club several years ago.

According to a formula in an article in Forbes Magazine my net worth would rank in the top 0.52% in the United States, which means it is likely similar for Canada.

http://www.forbes.com/sites/billions/2010/01/21/the-billionaire-formula/

Again, it doesn't make me rich, but it does put me near the top of the ladder in terms of net worth. I accumulated this money, not through inheritance, stock options or some other windfall. I earned it and I saved. I now have invested a sum of money that equals the sum total of all of my gross earnings since the day I got my first full time job in 1971 earning $325 per month. AND my long term annual return on investment is about 10%.

I have a good education, which has helped me get above average wages, but I have never been in the ultra-high income earning crowd. My wages have been modest compared to many of those who acquired similar education and experience.

So if an ordinary person like me can do this,

then why can't you? It's not magic.

At the time of writing this book, I have about fifty people who actively follow my investing strategy through a monthly blog I write. Each month I give a brief discussion of the markets for that month, my performance and my stock suggestions. Most of the blog followers just do what I do and are quite happy with the results. I will give my opinion, but I never advise people what to do. This is an open site available to anyone. I don't ask for people to sign up, although you are welcome to. I don't need to know who you are and I don't contact any of my followers unless they ask me to.

In this book I will outline my current (very successful) investment strategy and my results. I will also provide a high level overview of the markets and their history. I will discuss a variety of investment vehicles, such as stocks (recommended), bonds (not recommended), ETFs (recommended), mutual funds (not recommended), and real estate (not recommended). I will provide my personal assessment of each and back up my assertions with real facts - not just possibilities and hypothetical scenarios. I have also provided a biographical narrative of my various attempts at making a fast-buck, before I got serious and found out what real investing is all about. I'm sure many of you will identify with my fumbling attempts.

I have focused on the past ten years, but have gone further into history where appropriate. Wherever possible I have used December 31, 2014 as the end date for financial analysis.

Chapter 1 - Definition of Investing

Many people throw the term "investing" around as if it were a beach ball. They don't give any thought to the meaning behind the term. Have you ever heard: "I invested in a new car." "I'm thinking of investing in a gym membership." "She invested in art." These are all throw-away lines that have nothing to do with investing. Following are some accepted definitions of investing. I use the term "investing" in the spirit of these definitions, all of which refer to using your money to buy something that you expect will return your initial expenditure and provide a return during the period of time you own it.

***

Wikipedia:

http://en.wikipedia.org/wiki/Investment

In finance, investing is putting money into an asset with the expectation of capital appreciation, dividends, and/or interest earnings. This may or may not be backed by research and analysis. Most or all forms of investment involve some form of risk, such as investment in equities, property and even fixed interest securities which are subject, among other things, to inflation risk. It is indispensable for project investors to identify and manage the risks related to the investment.

***

<u>*Investopedia*</u>

http://www.investopedia.com/terms/i/investing.asp

An asset or item that is purchased with the hope that it will generate income or appreciate in the future.

***

Look up the term investing in any other source and you will get a similar definition.
***

Chapter 2 - My Results

I will start with a summary of my returns to establish my credibility.

The following table shows my returns for the past ten years. You will note that my average returns exceed both the Canadian and US Market, although my objective is not to beat the market. I measure my returns in Canadian dollars, while I have considerable investments in U.S. stocks. As a result my returns are inflated when the Canadian dollar is weak (as it is at the time of writing), and deflated when the Canadian dollar is strong.

So for example my 2014 returns show as over 19% when the actual stock prices only increased by just over 9% plus dividends of about 3% totalling nearly 12% return. You will see that my returns expressed in Canadian dollars were lower than the markets when the Canadian dollar was strong.

During this ten year period the Canadian dollar has fluctuated from below $0.70 US to over $1.10 US. I choose to measure in Canadian dollars as I live in Canada and will spend my money in Canadian dollars.

You will also see two columns labelled Return 1 and Return 2. I have provided this range to demonstrate the impact of putting new money into the portfolio. If you assume the money enters the pot early in the period, for example January, (Return 2) it will show a lower return than if you show the money entering later, for example December (Return 1) in the period. Either way, my results are very good. It is better to show the exact time new money enters (or money leaves) the portfolio, but for the average investor that just makes measurement more complicated and difficult, and it is important to measure your results.

You will see the impact in the markets of the crash of 2008-09 (see later commentary). My results do not show the same drop as the general market. The biggest explanation of my good fortune is the type of investments I select, while part is due to the impact of exchange rates, and part of it is the dumb luck of having an excess of uninvested cash at the start of the crash.

My results are not a flash in the pan. They are long term and sustainable. Ask yourself if you would like to have an average annual return of 10%? It certainly beats all available alternatives as you will see in the rest of this book.

The TSX and S&P are market indexes that are explained later. (See Chapter 7)

Brian's returns

	Return 1	**Return 2**	**TSX**	**S&P**
2014	19.23%	19.23%	7.42%	11.39%
2013	29.03%	26.45%	9.56%	29.60%
2012	13.60%	13.00%	4.00%	13.41%
2011	8.06%	6.13%	-11.07%	0.00%
2010	6.63%	6.18%	14.45%	12.78%
2009	-2.07%	-2.07%	30.69%	23.45%
2008	2.16%	1.98%	-35.03%	-38.49%
2007	-9.26%	-8.72%	7.16%	3.53%
2006	19.88%	15.26%	14.51%	13.62%
2005	16.98%	14.31%	21.91%	3.00%
Average	**10.42%**	**9.18%**	**6.36%**	**7.23%**

My Portfolio

I invest in stocks (shares in companies). There are many other forms of investment that I will discuss later in the book, but none provide the long term sustainable returns obtained in the stock market. I will back up all of my statements with actual facts and data, not hypothetical situations.

Each of the US stocks that I buy is rated A++ (top rating by ValueLine, an investment research company I use) and have a long history of paying dividends and a history of increasing dividends each year. My Canadian stocks fit a similar profile, but do not receive the same high rating by ValueLine.

Below is a list of the stocks I held as of December 31, 2014. There are 23 US stocks and 17

Canadian stocks for a total of 40 different stocks. I think that this is too many stocks and will start culling some of the lower performing stock during 2015 to reduce the total number of stocks I hold. I think for my size of portfolio, 30 to 35 stocks provide sufficient diversification. Any more just adds needless duplication.

<u>*Brian's Portfolio – December 31, 2014*</u>

US Stocks		Canadian Stocks	
Name	**Symbol**	**Name**	**Symbol**
ConocoPhillips	COP	BCE Inc.	BCE
Cisco Systems, Inc.	CSCO	Bank of Montreal	BMO
E I Du Pont De Nemours	DD	Bank of Nova Scotia	BNS
Intel Corporation	INTC	Canadian Imperial Bank of Commerce	CM
Johnson & Johnson	JNJ	Enbridge Inc	ENB
Kimberly Clark Corp	KMB	Fortis Inc	FTS
The Coca-Cola Co	KO	Great-West Lifeco Inc.	GWO
Lockheed Martin Corporation	LMT	Husky Energy Inc.	HSE
McDonald's Corporation	MCD	National Bank of Canada	NA

14

Altria Group Inc	MO	Power Financial Corp	PWF
Merck & Co., Inc.	MRK	Russel Metals Inc	RUS
Novartis AG (ADR)	NVS	Royal Bank of Canada	RY
Public Service Enterprise Group	PEG	TELUS Corporation	T
PepsiCo, Inc.	PEP	Toronto-Dominion Bank	TD
Pfizer Inc.	PFE	Thomson Reuters Corporation	TRI
Procter & Gamble Co	PG	TransCanada Corporation	TRP
Philip Morris International Inc.	PM		
Royal Dutch Shell plc (ADR)	RDS.A		
AT&T Inc.	T		
Total SA (ADR)	TOT		
Unilever plc (ADR)	UL		
Verizon Communications Inc.	VZ		

For the US stocks, all but two adhere strictly to the strategy I have outlined. The two that don't conform are MO and PM, two tobacco companies. I acquired these stocks when I was using the Dogs of the Dow strategy (see later section for explanation).

15

At that time Altria (MO) was one of the Dow Jones list of 30 companies that are meant to represent the US stock market. However MO split into two companies and was pulled from the Dow and replaced with another company. Neither company is ranked as A++ by ValueLine, but I chose to keep them both because of their high and growing dividend yield and they continue to provide capital appreciation. I will dispose of them in 2015 to maintain my investment discipline.

ValueLine does not rank any Canadian company as A++. Much of my cash is in Canadian dollars and for several years my income was in Canadian dollars. I don't like to convert between currencies, if I can help it, because you tend to lose every time and I am not in the currency speculation business. Therefore, I needed a similar approach for my Canadian cash, so I just lowered my threshold to ValueLine's B++ rating which is still quite good. I also backed up the picks by checking with various other publicly available ratings.

More on how you can do this yourself later in the book under DIY.

Dividends

In addition to the rating by ValueLine, my major criterion is dividends. I try to purchase stocks that have dividend yield of at least 3% yield.

Companies issue their dividends once, twice or four times per year. The dividend is declared and paid as dollars per share. You calculate a company's dividend yield by taking the dividends per share paid by the company and dividing that number by the current market price of those shares.

My current dividend yield:

Given that I generally do not purchase stocks with a dividend yield below 3%, my current yield on my portfolio is just under 4%. That means that using the market value of my stocks as a base, I receive cash payments in the amount of 4% of my total portfolio. For me, these cash payments alone provide me with sufficient income to live comfortably. All of the companies in my portfolio have a history of increasing their dividends each year, so I have built in inflation protection.

There is no need for me to sell stocks to raise cash on which to live. I can exist on the dividends alone and allow my portfolio to grow as the market grows.

Incidentally, as a Canadian resident paying taxes in Canada, I receive very favourable tax treatment on my Canadian stocks.

Chapter 3 - My Strategy

Here is a posting I made to my investment website a few years ago detailing my investment strategy and how I arrived at it. I have reprinted it as-is, unedited. It gives a good overview of my strategy.

The Strategy

I like investing and having control over my assets, but like many others, I do not have the time to spend hours analyzing individual stocks. So I look for a simple, easy to understand, low maintenance strategy that, hopefully will provide me with capital protection primarily, potential for future income, and perhaps even some growth. At my stage of life, capital preservation is my main objective. I don't have enough time left to recover from catastrophic losses and I don't need huge growth to meet my financial objectives.

James O'Shaughnessy provides investing strategies for those wanting to do their own investing. One of his major strategies calls for investing in strong companies with high dividends and high dividend growth. His analysis has shown that this strategy beats the market consistently over time. He uses Value Line, a fee based investment service, to assess companies.

1) Strength – O'Shaughnessy recommends only investing in the strongest companies. This addresses the objective of capital preservation. If you screen stocks traded on the NYSE, using the A++

rating, the highest strength rating, you will find a universe of only about 50 some stocks. This is no guarantee that these companies won't go bad (witness Citi Bank and Bank of America and others), but it certainly improves your odds of getting long lasting companies.

2) Dividends – O'Shaughnessy looks for companies that have a reasonably high dividend. The thinking is that the higher the dividend the more value there is in the stock. This is like the "Dogs of the Dow" strategy, but with a bigger universe of stocks. Still if you only take the top dividend payers, say greater than 2 ¼ %, you end up with a list of only about 30 stocks.

3) Dividend growth – O'Shaughnessy looks for companies that have consistently increased their dividends over a long period of time. This strategy allows for your return on your original investment to grow, which is better than an equivalent GIC that has a fixed annual return.

Using this strategy, I analyzed 30 stocks that meet these criteria. There are a couple stocks that don't quite fit, because their dividend growth is small, but I have included them anyway.

The first 10 years of the new millennium have been referred to as the lost decade. Returns over that period of time were dismal. If you invested a dollar in the year 2000 into the S&P, you would only have about 90 cents at the end of 10 years.

I have used the start of May in my analysis. I took the stock prices as of May 10, 2011 and compared them to May 1, 2010 (one year earlier), May 1, 2006 (5 years), and May 1, 2001 (10 years). I made the assumption that you purchased 100 shares of each of these 30 companies. This starts you with a total investment of about $147,000. I compared this against taking the same $147,000 and investing in an ETF that tracks the DJIA and the S&P 500.

Your broad, 30 stock investment would now be worth over $180,000. Now that only works out to about a 3% annual compound growth rate, which is nothing to write home about, but it is on the plus side – not too bad for the "lost decade". However when you also consider that these are dividend stocks, you would have received an average of over 3% in dividends each year, your annual returns are now over 6% over a 10 year period of no growth. You would have annual income of nearly $6,000 from dividends.

If you invested in a Dow Jones ETF, your $180,000 would only be worth $171,000 and the S&P would be less than $158,000. You have beaten the market and produce an acceptable return, with little effort, low risk, in a period of time when most people were losing money in the market.

If you take those 30 stocks and eliminate 10 with the lowest dividend growth rate and purchase 100 shares in each of the remaining 20 companies, you would have invested just over $93,000 and end up with over $116,000, again only about a 3% annual compound growth rate, but also a healthy dividend return giving you about 6% per year.

Compare this to the DJIA which would give you $109,000 or the S&P producing $101,000. The O'Shaughnessy strategy still outperforms.

This commentary is only meant to provide information, not advice. Each individual needs to determine their own financial goals, risk profile and select a strategy that works for them. This strategy works for me. My current portfolio is similar, but not identical to this. I have some stocks left over from a previous strategy, and I also have several Canadian companies that do not get screened in using ValueLine.

December 2010

Chapter 4 - Evolution of My Investment Strategy

Excerpt from my investing blog:

I wrote this blog entry in November 2011, three years before I retired, and have reprinted it here as-is. I feel it gives a good summary of how I got to where I am.

***

When you have no money, you don't spend a lot of time thinking about investing. I owned a house and as a result I had no money. As I would later learn, what most people never do, a house is a home, not an investment. It may make you feel wealthy, but it actually depletes your wealth. But that's a topic for another story. There are too many non-believers and most will never convert.

I simultaneously sold my house and received a severance package for leaving a long term employer and I was suddenly in a cash surplus position, something I had never experienced before, and as such, I was now an investor.

My first move was to do what most new investors do, accept an invitation from a local Investors Group mutual fund salesman to explain investing. Convinced by his vastly superior knowledge of the investment market, I purchased a variety of Investors Group mutual funds from Charles, who had recently been laid off from his employer, a common profile for this type of "expert". As this was the 1990's, the era of peace and prosperity, all investments thrived and my wealth increased and I was happy.

I moved away from the Investors Group when my new employer provided a local investment firm, run by a couple of old ladies, who did investing in mutual funds for employees of the company. My wealth continued to grow, mainly due to new savings, but at a considerably slower pace. At this point, many of the employees of the company began complaining about the lack of service and knowledge provided by the nice, but not too swift, senior citizens who passed themselves off as investment advisors. As controller of the company, I asked for, and received from the president, permission to seek a new investment firm that could satisfy the needs of the employees of the company. My wealth, although not vast, was growing and not being a home owner any more, I was amassing more new cash than I ever had in the past. I wanted to put this money to work effectively and I felt that the current situation was not effective and efficient.

After a search of several companies, I settled on a real investment company with a properly trained investment advisor and a full range of investments, not just mutual funds that benefit the salesman. The president of the company agreed and we began using the services of Nesbit Burns, which was the investment arm of the Bank of Montreal.

Through this move, I was able to work with my new investment advisor, who became a friend, to migrate away from mutual funds, which consume a disproportionate amount of the gains by way of the MER (management expense ratio – how the fund manager gets paid), and into direct stock investing. I used the expertise of my broker to select a range of stocks and fixed income vehicles that met my risk profile which was somewhat aggressive, given that I was in my early forties.

After departing the corporate world for my own consulting business, I took more direct control of my investment portfolio. I had migrated completely away from mutual funds and into direct stock investment. At this time the size of my portfolio was not really sufficient to take full advantage of diversification, so I elected to move more into ETF's (exchange traded funds). These instruments had much of the benefits of mutual funds, such as diversification, but did not have the high fees attached to them, and they traded like stocks. The biggest disadvantage was that you could select the type of profile the fund could have, but you could not select the exact companies. This was left up to the fund manager.

At this point I started to research the benefits of dividend paying companies and started to move into ETFs that held dividend stocks. Now my portfolio was getting large enough that I felt I could properly diversify myself and I started migrating away from ETFs and into dividend producing stocks. My main focus was on the current dividend yield and I didn't pay much attention to the other important components. I was looking for companies that had high dividends and were large, well-known companies.

It was then that I discovered the "Dogs of the Dow" strategy and started to use this method to help pick my stocks, although I didn't follow it religiously, I used it as a guideline but purchased many stocks that were not on the Dow. I even used the method to purchase European companies that were traded on the New York Stock Exchange. By 2007, several of these companies had performed much better than I ever expected and instead of letting them ride, I decided to take my profits and re-examine my strategy. As a result I ended up with over fifty percent of my portfolio in cash while I contemplated my next move, looking for good buying opportunities. The market started to slide, which made me feel there would be some good buys coming up. Then the slide turned into a rout and we had the big financial crisis on our hands, and I was flush with cash – more luck than brains.

I sat out the crash with my portfolio never falling more than fifteen percent from its peak and when it appeared to be over, and I felt it was safe to go back into the water, I started buying again. But now I was using a much stricter and more disciplined approach.

I purchased only strong companies as defined by ValueLine and only those that had a dividend of greater than 2.5% and a long history of increasing their dividends. Research has shown these types of stocks outperform the market in the long run.

My objective is to build a portfolio that produces enough dividends for me to live off in retirement. Hopefully the stocks will also grow, but I don't want to have to rely on the growth for my income. Although in the short run other strategies may produce better overall returns, I am finding that in the long run, this approach continues to outperform the market and outperform other strategies touted by various gurus, who come and go more often than boy-bands.

My portfolio consists of stocks that I purchased starting as early as 2004, but because of my purchase and subsequent sales during the 2005 to 2008 time period has resulted in the bulk of my current portfolio being acquired from January 2010 onwards.

Other than a couple of bad acquisitions that I didn't get rid of early enough (eg General Electric, Great West Life), my older purchases have had outstanding performance and my 2010 purchases are doing great. But they all produce dividends and the current yield on my overall portfolio is almost 4%, before any capital appreciation.

I am now well on my way to having enough dividends to provide a comfortable retirement, before accessing my capital gains, or depleting my capital.

Chapter 5 - Suggested Stocks

Using the criteria of an "A++" rating by ValueLine, a positive dividend yield and a ten year record of increasing dividends, there is only a small universe of stocks to select from. As of the writing of this book, that list includes only the sixty-four stocks listed below. A rating of A++ by ValueLine indicates that these companies have passed all the necessary strength tests. If by chance one were to drop to the ValueLine A+ rating, it would still be a good company not requiring any panic selling, however I almost always sell when the rating drops, just to maintain my portfolio discipline. Changes to the rating are rare. For my portfolio, because I rely on it for my income, I only pick stocks with a dividend yield above 3%. The further you are away from retirement, the lower the yield you need and can select based on capital appreciation potential. However, I still recommend going with the higher yield stocks as the core portfolio. Capital appreciation is when the stock goes up in value – eg from $25 per share to $35 per share. Dividend yield is the dividends per share divided by the share price.

Top 10 yield (note: this list is heavily weighted to oil, given the low price of oil at the time of writing this book). This list is as of December 31, 2014. Although it doesn't change much or often, there are some changes over time, so if you are looking to adopt this strategy, consult a more current list at my blog.

Company	Ticker	Dividend Yield	Dividend Growth 10-Year
Royal Dutch Shell 'B'	RDSB	5.55	6.50
AT&T Inc.	T	5.45	4.00
Total ADR	TOT	5.29	13.00
Verizon Communic.	VZ	4.46	3.00
Chevron Corp.	CVX	4.00	9.50
Occidental Petroleum	OXY	3.87	15.50
Public Serv. Enterprise	PEG	3.70	2.50
Unilever PLC ADR	UL	3.43	9.00
McDonald's Corp.	MCD	3.42	25.50
Emerson Electric	EMR	3.25	7.00

Total List

Company	Ticker	Dividend Yield	Dividend Growth 10-Year
3M Company	MMM	2.42	6.50
Abbott Labs.	ABT	2.02	5.00
AT&T Inc.	T	5.45	4.00
Automatic Data Proc.	ADP	2.32	13.50
Baxter Int'l Inc.	BAX	3.03	10.00
Becton, Dickinson	BDX	1.62	16.50
Boeing	BA	2.40	11.50
Bristol-Myers Squibb	BMY	2.41	2.00
Cardinal Health	CAH	1.65	26.00
Chevron Corp.	CVX	4.00	9.50
Chubb Corp.	CB	1.99	9.00
Coca-Cola	KO	3.11	10.00
Colgate-Palmolive	CL	2.14	12.50
Deere & Co.	DE	2.63	15.50
Disney (Walt)	DIS	1.10	13.50
Dover Corp.	DOV	2.21	9.50
Du Pont	DD	2.46	2.00
Emerson Electric	EMR	3.25	7.00
Exxon Mobil Corp.	XOM	3.22	8.50
Fluor Corp.	FLR	1.45	6.50
Franklin Resources	BEN	1.16	15.00
Gen'l Dynamics	GD	1.78	13.00
Grainger (W.W.)	GWW	1.80	15.50
Home Depot	HD	2.05	19.50

Honeywell Int'l	HON	2.00	7.50
Illinois Tool Works	ITW	1.95	12.00
Infosys Ltd. ADR	INFY	1.59	31.50
Intel Corp.	INTC	2.85	26.50
Int'l Business Mach.	IBM	2.83	19.00
Johnson & Johnson	JNJ	2.72	11.50
Kimberly-Clark	KMB	3.20	8.50
Lockheed Martin	LMT	2.98	22.50
McDonald's Corp.	MCD	3.42	25.50
McKesson Corp.	MCK	0.42	13.00
Medtronic plc	MDT	1.61	15.50
Merck & Co.	MRK	3.05	1.50
Microsoft Corp.	MSFT	2.81	28.00
NIKE, Inc. 'B'	NKE	1.16	18.50
Northrop Grumman	NOC	1.68	11.50
Novartis AG ADR	NVS	2.68	15.50
Novo Nordisk ADR	NVO	1.89	28.50
Occidental Petroleum	OXY	3.87	15.50
PepsiCo, Inc.	PEP	2.74	13.50
Pfizer, Inc.	PFE	3.24	5.50
Precision Castparts	PCP	0.06	7.00
Procter & Gamble	PG	3.03	10.50
Public Serv. Enterprise	PEG	3.70	2.50
Qualcomm Inc.	QCOM	2.33	29.50

Raytheon Co.	RTN	2.23	10.50
Royal Dutch Shell 'B'	RDSB	5.55	6.50
Schlumberger Ltd.	SLB	2.38	11.50
Sigma-Aldrich	SIAL	0.67	16.00
Smucker (J.M.)	SJM	2.25	10.00
Stryker Corp.	SYK	1.46	32.00
Texas Instruments	TXN	2.29	25.00
TJX Companies	TJX	1.03	23.50
Total ADR	TOT	5.29	13.00
Travelers Cos.	TRV	2.04	4.50
Unilever PLC ADR	UL	3.43	9.00
Union Pacific	UNP	1.82	20.50
United Technologies	UTX	2.09	15.00
UnitedHealth Group	UNH	1.32	58.50
Verizon Communic.	VZ	4.46	3.00
Wal-Mart Stores	WMT	2.34	18.00

I run this list regularly and post it on my blog:

https://borgfordinvesting.wordpress.com/

Chapter 6 - DIY - How can I do it myself?

One way or another you are probably invested in the stock market whether you know it or not. Most people have either a company pension, or an individual retirement fund (RRSP or IRA). If you happen to be an ex-pat working in a foreign country, you are probably spinning off excess cash and are wondering what to do with it. If you are in this latter category you have probably already succumbed to the one of the many sycophants selling a variety of mutual funds or you have decided to park your money in real estate. As discussed later, real estate is a poor investment alternative, and mutual funds, especially those hawked by hucksters in less regulated markets, are losers.

I'm not trying to convince you to do what I have done. That is purely your choice. If you do want to do this or something similar, it is not that difficult, anyone can do it. Below are the basic steps you would need to do to get started.

1) **Have a bank account**. You need to have a place to put your money, transact your daily affairs and as a source for funding your investment account. If you are in Canada, any of the big five (six including National Bank) are fine. I have an account at ScotiaBank but I rely more on HSBC because my international experience convinced me that it is one of the few truly international banks. I love the big six banks in Canada as a place to invest, but they don't

know and don't care about anything to do with customer service. They cater to their shareholders and shun their customers. As an investor in all six banks, I'm OK with that.

If you are in the U.S., any of the big banks are good places to put your money for everyday transaction purposes.

If you are an ex-pat, especially if you are living in the Middle East, you need to select a bank that is trusted world-wide and is not associated with money laundering or terrorism. Most local banks are tainted and transfers from those banks may not be accepted. HSBC, CitiBank and Standard Chartered are usually acceptable choices. Again I found HSBC to be exceptional when it comes to moving money internationally.

2) **Open an investment account**. In Canada, every one of the big banks has a good discount brokerage company. Again, I use HSBC InvestDirect, which is rated below those of the banks, but is still very good.

In the U.S. any discount on-line brokerage firm is good. This includes TD Ameritrade, Charles Schwab or any other well-known name.

The best firm I found internationally was TD Direct Investing in Luxembourg (formerly Internaxx). It has high trading fees, but you shouldn't be trading frequently anyway. It is very reliable and provides good service. However there are some countries that it won't do business with, such as Turkey, in which case you would have to find another choice. KeyTrade, also out of Luxembourg seems to be a good alternative but I have no direct experience with it. You can also use HSBC out of the UK Channel Islands, but it is very restrictive on how often and where you can trade.

3) **Fund your trading account**. Find an easy way to transfer money from your bank to your trading account. Most banks have a simple on-line transfer mechanism, but in some cases you might have to write cheques.

4) **Start trading**. Learn how to move around the website provided by your brokerage company. They are all easy to maneuver, but each one is slightly different from the others.

When buying you will place a buy order with the quantity of shares you want to buy and the ticker symbol. Make sure you do the calculation of how many shares you can buy with the money you have allotted to the purchase. I normally trade in at least $10,000 blocks in order to keep my trading costs down, but with the discount brokerages, the fees are quite low, often well under $10 per trade. I would not bother trading in amounts below $5,000 however. When trading during the trading day, I just place a market order, which means that I will buy at whatever the going price is. You can, however put in a limit price where the trade will not proceed until the price drops to whatever level you place. If trading after hours I always use the limit pricing, Which means just putting a share price limit close to the range of the last trading price. This just prevents someone from putting in a goofy number, perhaps a high price to sell and you end up buying too high compared to market. I have never been burned, nor have I heard of anyone being burned on high volume stocks, but I have heard of it on low volume stocks and I wouldn't take the chance.

When selling you will place a sell order for the number of shares you want to sell and insert the ticker symbol for your stock. Then again you can place a market or a limit order. You use a limit order if you don't want to sell below a certain price. I use that for after-hours trading or if I want to ensure I get my price. However if the market never reaches that price, your trade will never execute.

There may be other tick boxes you may have to click before you finish and some on-line brokers require that you have a trading PIN, which is just another level of security to make sure you are doing what you actually want to do. Once a trade executes you cannot reverse it, so look at your information carefully before clicking the final button.

5) **Track your portfolio**. There is a saying in quality control, "What gets measured gets done." If you monitor your portfolio and measure your results that tends to improve your decisions and lets you know how effective you are being. Remember this is a long-term strategy so don't be too overjoyed with short term gains nor should you panic with short term losses. You need to be tracking your annual return on your portfolio and comparing it to other measures. You don't need to beat the market on the upside, but you sure don't want to be exceeding the market on the downside. That's the objective of this conservative

strategy - protect capital and provide income.

I have provided my contact information and my website address if anyone feels the need to contact me for assistance. I don't run a business and I don't charge for my help.

brianborgford@hotmail.com

https://borgfordinvesting.wordpress.com/

Chapter 7 - Markets, Terminology and Investment Instruments

The Markets

When I refer to markets, I am talking about three stock indexes - TSX, DJIA, S&P 500. What are they you ask?

TSX (formerly known as the TSE) - The Toronto Stock Exchange has about 4,000 publicly listed companies. The TSX composite index takes over 200 stocks and through a consistent weighting process provides a number that gives a reasonable representation of how the Canadian stock market in general is performing.

DJIA - Dow Jones Industrial Average is a weighted average of 30 of the top industrial stock prices in the United States. The companies included in this list are not static, as companies are added and deleted occasionally. It is intended to give a picture of how the New York Stock Exchange (NYSE) is performing.

S&P 500 - Standard and Poor's 500 index includes the largest 500 American companies traded on the NYSE and the NASDQ exchange (which tends to include more technology companies). It is considered a better measure of the US stock market as it has a broader range of companies than the DJIA, but the two indexes tend to move nearly identically.

There are many other indexes that can be used to measure market performance, but these are the ones that are used the most. I will refer to these three indexes in my analysis.

In addition to stock markets, there are other markets including the bond market, money market, commodities market, and others. I will take a brief look at bonds, but I will not address any of the other markets as they are not for the faint of heart and require considerable expertise. Even the experts don't usually do well in these other markets over time.

Terminology

Generally when someone starts throwing a bunch of technical investing terms at you, it is them trying to impress you on how much they know. This is often done by investment advisors to demonstrate how much better off you would be in placing your money with them. When you start hearing too many of these investment terms, run for the hills. These terms will be used over and over again to help them explain to you why your returns are not what you expected them to be. I am not interested in terminology; I'm interested in returns.

That said there are a few terms that are useful to understand.

Price Earnings ratio (PE ratio) - this is calculated by dividing the current market price of the shares by its EPS (earnings per share). It represents the market's perception of the future profits of the company. Generally the lower the number the better, but some industries have lower numbers than other industries. Once you start to exceed a number of 20, you need to beware.

Liquidity - for your purposes it represents the speed with which you can convert your investment into cash. For example, a frequently traded stock like MCD (McDonald's Restaurants) is highly liquid in that you can get your cash out with an on line trade. At the other extreme is real estate which can take years to convert into cash and as such is considered illiquid. I prefer high liquidity for my investments.

Yield on Cost - this represents the dividends per share divided by the share price you actually paid for your stock. For shares in companies that have had growing value, this number can be quite high as you will see in my later analysis. This can be a very useful number in comparing stock investments to other fixed income investments such as term deposits.

ADR - American Deposit Receipt. Don't worry about the technical explanation of this term. All you need to know is that this is how foreign companies can trade their shares on the US stock markets. Examples include Unilever and Royal Dutch Shell.

Dividends - The amount of the company's profits they have decided to distribute to shareholders as cash, stated in dollars per share.

Dividend Yield - The company's dividend (dollars per share) divided by the current share price.

Share Price - how many dollars it costs to purchase one share of a company's stock. This can be found daily on any financial website.

Earnings per share - the company's net profit divided by the number of shares outstanding.

Yahoo Finance has a very comprehensive glossary of financial terminology, most of which you will never need.

http://biz.yahoo.com/f/g/g.html

ETFs - Exchange Traded Funds

I advocate buying individual stocks and have the results to support that approach. If you are absolutely opposed to owning individual stocks, the next best approach, and many would argue an even better approach, is using ETFs or Exchange Traded Funds. As a matter of fact this is the method that Warren Buffet recommends for new investors, and even seasoned investors and I would not bet against Warren Buffet. My portfolio has often performed better than equivalent ETFs, but not always.

Exchange Traded Funds have all of the positive features of mutual funds (discussed next) and almost none of the poor features. On the other hand, ETFs trade just like an individual stock making it highly liquid.

An ETF is a basket of stocks usually resembling the stocks in a specific index like the DJIA, S&P, TSX or many others. They are very efficient in that they mirror almost exactly the exchange they represent. There is a management fee associated with ETFs but it is very small compared to a mutual fund and the gains in the ETF seem to exceed the management fee making the fees virtually unnoticeable.

Here is what Yahoo Finance says about ETFs:

http://finance.yahoo.com/glossary-e/

"Exchange-traded funds (ETFs) are listed on a stock exchange and trade like stock. You can use traditional stock trading techniques, such as stop orders, limit orders, margin purchases, and short sales when you buy or sell ETFs. But ETFs also resemble mutual funds in some ways. For example, you buy shares of the fund, which in turn owns a portfolio of stocks. Each ETF has a net asset value (NAV), which is determined by the total market capitalization of the stocks in the portfolio, plus dividends but minus expenses, divided by the number of shares issued by the fund. ETF prices change throughout the trading day, in response to supply and demand, rather than just at the end of the trading day as open-end mutual fund prices do. The market price and the NAV are rarely the same, but the differences are typically small. That's due to a unique process that allows institutional investors to buy or redeem large blocks of shares at the NAV with in-kind baskets of the fund's stocks."

Mutual Funds

As defined in Yahoo Finance

http://biz.yahoo.com/f/g/mm.html

"Mutual funds are pools of money that are managed by an investment company and regulated by the Investment Company Act of 1940. They offer investors a variety of goals, depending on the fund and its investment charter. Some funds seek to generate income on a regular basis. Others seek to preserve an investor's money. Still others seek to invest in companies that are growing at a rapid pace. Funds can impose a sales charge, or load, on investors when they buy or sell shares. No-load funds impose no sales charge."

***

A mutual fund is comprised of stocks, bonds or other instruments as defined by the fund's mandate. For the record, I am not a fan of mutual funds for reasons stated below. They are run by a fund manager who is usually assigned this role by an investment company, this could be a bank, investment firm or some other such organization.

My reasons for not liking mutual funds:

1) *Performance* - the vast majority of mutual funds under-perform the markets and often by a considerable amount. Those funds that do outperform the market seldom do so for any sustained period, usually only a year or two. Those that do have a

somewhat sustained level of performance will usually only comprise a small portion of any investor's portfolio making the superior performance insignificant in their overall returns.

2) *Sales charges* - many funds require you to pay an upfront commission to the salesman or broker making your initial investment smaller than you expected, thus reducing your returns. Some funds have no upfront sales charge but require you to pay a penalty upon withdrawing any funds, again eating into any potential returns.

3) *Management fees* (MER or Management Expense Ratio) - every mutual fund makes money for the firm it represents and for the fund manager regardless of whether the fund gains or loses money. This is due to a fee they withdraw from the fund every year to pay for their expenses and to provide them with a profit. Often these fees are as low as 2% or less, but I have seen them well above 3%. Although you don't pay this directly, your fund returns are severely hurt by these fees. In addition, some funds, especially European funds, have a fee (often about 1% per year) that is charged directly to you.

4) *Liquidity* - you cannot convert your investment in mutual funds into cash as quickly as you can with stocks or ETFs. If you operate through a broker, you must contact the broker with a sell order, who, in turn contacts the fund manager, who must then sell securities to cover the cash that you

have requested. This can take days to weeks or even longer depending on the nature of the fund and the efficiency or desire of the broker and investment firm. Then you are subject to their withdrawal penalty. I witnessed one co-worker lose over 60% of their investment in a long term exotic mutual fund when they tried to redeem and get out of a sticky commitment, bordering on a scam. This is the exception, but beware.

If you are not convinced of the pitfalls of mutual funds, do some research on the funds you are planning to buy. The main reason people purchase mutual funds is that they are easy to buy and require no thinking or analysis. Often you can buy them from the comfort of your own home with the help of an only too willing sales person sitting on your sofa filling out the plethora of required documentation on your behalf.

Here is one article on mutual funds. Do your own search and read about the perils and pitfalls of mutual funds. If you find a positive review, check to see who the author is and if they have anything to gain.

http://www.nytimes.com/2015/03/04/business/americans-arent-saving-enough-for-retirement-but-one-change-could-help.html?action=click&contentCollection=U.S.&module=MostEmailed&version=Full&region=Marginalia&src=me&pgtype=article&_r=0

Excerpt from the article:

A research paper by Mr. Bogle published in

Financial Analysts Journal makes the case. Actively managed mutual funds, in which many workers invest their retirement savings, are enormously costly.

First, there is the expense ratio — about 1.12 percent of assets for the average large capitalization blend fund. Then there are transaction costs and distribution costs. Active funds also pay a penalty for keeping a share of their assets in low-yielding cash. Altogether, costs add up to 2.27 percent per year, Mr. Bogle estimates.

By contrast, a passive index fund, like Vanguard's Total Stock Market Index Fund, costs merely 0.06 percent a year in all.

Of course, Mr. Bogle has a horse in the race. He founded the Vanguard Group. He invented the first index fund for the public. His case is powerful, nonetheless.

Assuming an annual market return of 7 percent, he says, a 30-year-old worker who made $30,000 a year and received a 3 percent annual raise could retire at age 70 with $927,000 in the pot by saving 10 percent of her wages every year in a passive index fund. (Such a nest egg, at the standard withdrawal rate of 4 percent, would generate an inflation-adjusted $37,000 a year more or less indefinitely.) If she put it in a typical actively managed fund, she would end up with only $561,000.

Bonds

Bonds are debt instruments issued by companies or governments. Companies will "borrow" money from investors with a promise to pay a stated interest payment (coupon rate) every year for a set number of years (often 10, 20 or 30 years) and at maturity they will pay you the face value of the bond - $1,000.

Depending on the coupon rate compared to current interest rates, the bond may trade above (at a premium), or below (at a discount) to the face value of $1,000.

You, the investor, can buy these bonds through a broker in the secondary market (i.e., from someone who already owns the bond) and you can later sell it through the same process. If you buy a bond at a discount, your yield will be greater than the coupon rate. If you buy at a premium, your return is less than the coupon rate.

Bond prices (market value) can go up and down during the life of the bond. Therefore, in addition to the interest you receive, you may incur a capital gain or a capital loss if you sell during the life of the bond.

Although I understand all the technical aspects of bonds, I am not comfortable enough with their market movement, so I do not trade in bonds myself. Also the interest rates have been so low in recent years that bonds do not provide an attractive return. Most investment advisors will tell you to maintain a certain percentage of your portfolio in bonds (usually 30 to 40 percent). I maintain a 30% weighting in my

RRSP (similar to the U.S. IRA) managed portfolio, but it is important to remember that bonds do not guarantee a return of your principal. If you hold them to maturity and the bond issuer does not default, you will likely get all of your principal back. If the interest rates rise, and you sell your bond, or if the bond issuer defaults, you may get back only a portion or even none of your principal.

Another class of bonds is government issued bonds which are considered relatively guaranteed. You may recall, however, when New York defaulted on their bonds, or when the U.S. reached their debt ceiling and were threatening to default. Many foreign countries have defaulted on their bonds with Greece being the most recent to threaten default.

I would recommend if you do decide to invest in bonds to do so through a qualified and knowledgeable broker or advisor. One of the few times I would recommend a broker or advisor.

Chapter 8 - Go International

Excerpt from my blog - April 2014

"You have to diversify your investment. Don't rely on only one country. Think of developing or emerging markets." How often do you hear that mantra? Again it is often spouted by those who are selling such instruments that propose to offer international exposure. And again I ask, "Show me your portfolio and returns." Seldom is there a response.

How well do you know these emerging and developing markets? What do you know about their stock exchanges and associated rule and regulations? Having lived in China, as much as I loved the experience, it taught me that this would not be a good place to put your money. Yes many of the developing economies are doing great, as are companies and businesses that operate within them, but how do actual individual investors do, especially in the long run?

I think that prudent international exposure is a good thing but what better way to do it than from the sanctuary of reasonably controlled and regulated market places. With all its flaws that are often exposed through frauds, the NYSE still is the most tightly controlled market in the world. Many of the large US based companies derive much of their income from emerging and developing markets. In addition, many non-US companies trade their shares on the NYSE through ADRs, which stands for American Deposit Receipts, which is just a method for international companies to raise equity through the NYSE.

HERE is an article on the value of going international with domestic stocks:

http://seekingalpha.com/article/3200776-international-diversification-may-be-closer-than-you-think?ifp=0&app=1

Here are some examples of US stocks traded on the NYSE that have heavy international exposure based on 2012 annual reports:

Conoco Philips (COP)- 50% of revenues from non US operations.

Coca Cola (KO) – 55 % of revenues from outside of North America and almost 60 % outside of the US.

McDonald's (MCD) – almost 70 % of its revenues come from outside the US.

3M (MMM) – produces 65% of its revenues from outside the US.

Merk (MRK) – almost 60% of its revenues come from outside the US.

Dupont (DD) has active operations in 90 countries.

Kimberley-Clark – KMB receives half of its revenues outside the US.

Johnson and Johnson (JNJ) gets over half of its revenue from outside the US.

***

The following companies are based in other countries but are traded on the NYSE using ADR:

Novartis (NVS) is a pharmaceutical company based in Switzerland.

Royal Dutch Shell (RDS-A) is an international oil and gas company headquartered in the Netherlands.

Total (TOT) is an international oil and gas company headquartered in Paris.

Unilever (UL) is located in London, UK providing consumer goods worldwide.

***

You will find if you go through most of the companies listed on my suggested list that a high percentage of their operations are outside the United States. How much more international diversification can you get? Would you rather have your international exposure managed under the auspices of the New York Stock Exchange, or would you be happy to take your chances with the Dubai Financial Market, or the Hang Seng out of Shanghai, or a market regulated in Nigeria, or Mumbai or Dhaka? Think about that when some uninformed observer advises you that you must go international or you will miss opportunities around the world. Again, ask them what their track record is – you likely won't get a response.

Chapter 9 - Types of Investors and Strategies

Following are some strategies used by investors. There are many variations, but I have just hit the highlights.

Dogs of the Dow

http://www.dogsofthedow.com/

This is an investing strategy that became popular a number of years ago. It only selects stocks from the Dow Jones 30 stocks. The concept is that those stocks with the highest dividend yields are the best value and likely have a suppressed share price allowing for an abnormal capital gain. You pick a point in time, eg Dec 31, and purchase the 10 highest yielding stocks on that date. Then on the same date the next year, you select the 10 highest yielding stocks at that time, sell the stocks that you currently own that aren't in that list of 10 (presumably at a profit) and round out by purchasing the ones you don't have, giving you 10 stocks in your portfolio for the next year when you do it all again.

There is a partner strategy that selects only the lowest share priced stocks and only selects 5 stocks.

When this strategy first appeared, year after year it beat the DJIA until one year it missed and it has been hit and miss ever since.

I used a variation of this strategy leading up to my current strategy. It served me well but had its limitations causing me to seek out a better approach.

I am not an advocate of this strategy, but there are still those who stick by it.

Buy the Dips

Buy the Dips is a strategy of making your purchases when one of your target stocks drops in price. Many investors have done will with this strategy, which is nothing more than an attempt at market timing.

I would definitely advocate for this method of purchasing as long as you are targeting stocks with a solid track record and generally employ a buy and hold strategy. You have to buy anyway, so you might as well try to buy at the best price possible - as I have mentioned elsewhere, I try to time the market, with limited success, but at least the action results in a purchase of a stock that belongs in my portfolio.

Conservative Investing

This is an attempt to invest only in those instruments that have the highest probability of preserving your capital.

Conservative investing, when understood and applied properly, is not a low-risk, low-return strategy. Investors must understand two definitions to appreciate the appropriate means by which to invest conservatively.

1. A *conservative investment* is one that carries the greatest likelihood of preserving the purchasing power of one's capital with the

least amount of risk.
2. *Conservative investing* is the understanding of what a conservative investment is, and then following a specific course of action needed to properly determine whether or not particular investments are indeed conservative investments. Government bonds are a good example of a conservative investment.

http://www.investopedia.com/articles/basics/09/be-a-conservative-investor.asp

Aggressive Investing

A portfolio management strategy that attempts to maximize returns by taking a relatively higher degree of risk. An aggressive investment strategy emphasizes capital appreciation as a primary investment objective, rather than income or safety of principal. Such a strategy would therefore have an asset allocation with a substantial weighting in stocks, and a much smaller allocation to fixed income and cash. Aggressive investment strategies are especially suitable for young adults because their lengthy investment horizon enables them to ride out market fluctuations better than investors with a short investment horizon. Regardless of the investor's age, however, a high tolerance for risk is an absolute prerequisite for an aggressive investment strategy.

http://www.investopedia.com/terms/a/aggressiveinvestmentstrategy.asp

Growth Investing

This is a strategy whereby an investor seeks out stocks with what they deem good growth potential. In most cases a growth stock is defined as a company whose earnings are expected to grow at an above-average rate compared to its industry or the overall market.

http://www.investopedia.com/terms/g/growthinvesting.asp

Growth investing is a style of investment strategy. Those who follow this style, known as *growth investors*, invest in companies that exhibit signs of above-average growth, even if the share price appears expensive in terms of metrics such as price-to-earnings or price-to-book ratios. In typical usage, the term "growth investing" contrasts with the strategy known as value investing.

However, some notable investors such as Warren Buffett have stated that there is no theoretical difference between the concepts of value and growth (*"Growth and Value Investing are joined at the hip"*), in consideration of the concept of an asset's intrinsic value. In addition, when just investing in one style of stocks, diversification could be negatively impacted.

Thomas Rowe Price, Jr. has been called "the father of growth investing".[1]

http://en.wikipedia.org/wiki/Growth_investing

Dividend Investing

This is generally investing in high yield stocks. Although it sounds good to invest in stocks that have a high current yield, this strategy in its simplest form does not take into consideration this history of the dividends, the sustainability of future dividends and the general strength of the company itself. I used this strategy at one time (see later examples) and had some success, but several failures. The biggest problem with this strategy is that it doesn't consider the strength of the company or the sustainability of the dividend. I got burned when companies eliminated or cut their dividends.

Dividend Growth Strategy

This is my strategy. I look for top quality stocks that have a good dividend and a strong track record of increasing their dividends which is a reasonable predictor of future increases. This strategy has the additional benefit of providing capital appreciation that seems to tag along with these strong companies. They tend to keep a relatively constant dividend yield which can only happen if the stock price increases at the same rate as the dividend increases.

Value Investing

Value investing means trying to buy stocks when they are undervalued and therefore you can expect larger than market gains when the stock price goes up. True value investing requires intense analysis and a strong technical understanding to make it work. There are some experienced investors who have made this work to their advantage - most notably, Warren Buffet.

I have met people who claim to be value investors, but they usually have no understanding of the stock market, companies and finance. They just like to toss out a term to make them sound knowledgeable. As a result they never actually do the detailed analysis required to be a successful value investor. What they are really doing is a cursory look at market trends for particular stocks and making a guess as to a good time to buy. This is little more than a crude attempt at market timing.

Everyone tries to time the market - it is only human nature to want to get a bargain. I try it myself. No one is ever successful at sustained market timing, so most of the self-proclaimed value investors never do match the market. One such value investor confided in me that his long term returns using his version of value investing, was only about 2%.

A prime example of this phenomenon is computer giant, Hewlitt-Packard (HPQ). In 2011, well after the crash, HP had declined from a high of almost $54 to Just over $30. My value investor associate couldn't resist this golden opportunity with one of the Dow Jones companies, and bought, proudly proclaiming his value purchase. HP continued on its downward spiral until it bottomed out at under $13 in late 2013. HP started a slow climb up to the point where after being invested in the company for three years he could claim that he was now in a break even position - the share price was now equal to what he had paid, during which time the DJIA grew by over 50%.

My value investor friend had annual returns of around 2% per year while mine was above 8% - this period of time included the 2008-09 crash.

Chapter 10 - Calculating Returns

As an investor it is important for me to know how my portfolio is performing, so I need to calculate my returns. However, how do you actually calculate your returns? And how do you account for any new money added to the pot or money taken out?

There are several ways to calculate returns and no one way is the absolute correct way. The important thing is to be consistent. I try to be consistent in how I measure my returns and try to be consistent when I compare my returns to other investments.

I am always comparing my returns to the market and to other returns, such as real estate. This constant measuring allows me to tell if I am doing OK and whether I need to adjust my methods at all. This is how I have ended up with my current strategy and migrated away from other strategies.

The simplest method of calculating a return is by taking the ending value, dividing by the beginning value, deduct "1" to account for the beginning value and convert to a percentage by multiplying by 100. For example if you start the year with $100 and end with $117, you divide 117 by 100, deduct 1 and multiply by 100 giving you 17%.

This works well for one period such as a month or even a year, as you always want to show your returns on an annual basis. One complication arises when you either add or deduct money during that period. The easiest way around that is to assume the money was added or removed either at the beginning of the period or at the end of the period - but you need to be consistent in how you apply this.

When you are trying to measure your return over multiple years it becomes a bit more complicated. You can simply average the returns adding the annual numbers and dividing by the number of years which gives you a good indicator of your average annual returns. This method does not, however, account for compounding (CAGR - explained next) so be careful to not confuse the two.

In my analysis of the various markets and other investments, I will try to show various methods of calculating returns for comparative purposes.

Compound Annual Growth Rate (CAGR)

You have likely heard this term or have heard it referred to as compounding. In simple terms it is earning interest (or returns) on your interest. For example if you invest $100 at 5% per year, you will have $105 after one year. Using simple interest you will have $110 after two years. But using compounding you will have $110.25. You will have earned the 5% not only on your original investment, but also on your earnings. Over time, this compounding becomes quite significant. After 10 years using simple interest, your savings will be $5 per year times 10 years plus your original $100 giving you $150. However using compounding you will have $162.89 or over 8 1/2% more. This is an important concept to understand in investing as will become apparent in later analysis.

Not to bore you with all the mathematical calculations to measure CAGR, here is a simple formula that I use to calculate CAGR:

$$CAGR = \left(\frac{\text{Ending Value}}{\text{Beginning Value}}\right)^{\left(\frac{1}{\text{\# of years}}\right)} - 1$$

If you plug the numbers used from above - ending value of 162.89, beginning value of 100, 10 year - you will get a CAGR of 5%.

***

How a difference in returns can affect your financial security.

If you invest $1,000 per year for 30 years at 6%, you will end up with $69,500. If you can get 1% more bringing your investment to a 7% yield, you would have over $83,000 or 20% more. If you were to accumulate $500,000 by the time you retire, think about the impact of that differential in returns. Twenty percent of $500,000 is $100,000. If you were to turn that 6% into 8% you would have 46% more or a quarter of a million more - almost $750,000. Think long and hard about your investment returns as they can make a huge difference in the long run.

Actual Returns

Now let's take a look at how actual investments have performed over the years.

Toronto Stock Exchange

As of December 31, 2014 the TSX index was 14,632,40. You can get the TSX (or other market) data from any one of a number of websites. I tend to use Yahoo Finance as it provides easy to find historical data on market and individual stocks.

In 2014, the TSX rose 7.48%. I get that by summing the individual monthly returns. If you compare the beginning balance (13,621.60) to the ending balance you will get 7.42%. The difference in calculations is insignificant for our purposes.

That is one year of returns, but I am not investing for one year; I invest for the long term. What are the long term returns for the TSX? And how long is long term? I used the data from Yahoo Finance which goes back to 1979, or 35 years. You could use longer time frames, but the numbers wouldn't vary that much.

The TSX at the end of 1979 was 1,813.20 compared to the number above of 14,632.40. This is the type of comparison most people do when looking at returns, especially housing prices. On this basis, the TSX has risen over 700% or over 20% per year on average. This is not a very realistic number for return calculations.

A better method would be to average the

monthly increases and multiply by 12 giving an average annual return on the TSX of 7.51%. If you average the 35 years, you get 7.35% which is almost the same - or close enough for our purposes. Therefore the long term return on the TSX is about 7-1/2%.

However if you consider compounding and use the formula for CAGR, you will get a smaller number of 6.15%. But that assumes that there is no money going in or out during that period.

I also looked at the returns over just the last 10 years (which included the big crash) and the average annual return is 6.36%. Using CAGR it would be 4.70% per year, but again that assumes no change to the pot.

So there are your TSX returns for the past 10 years (6.36%) and for the past 35 years (7 1/2%). This can now form the basis for evaluating your Canadian returns.

XIU - Canadian Market ETF

Of course you can't actually purchase shares of TSX as it is just an index of all of the stocks it represents. But you can buy an ETF (see previous discussion on ETFs) that tries to match the exact performance of the TSX by buying and selling shares in order to always approximate the weightings of the stocks on the Canadian market index. One such ETF trades under the ticker symbol XIU.

XIU has a 15 year compound annual growth rate of about 5.6% including dividends which is very close to the returns for the same period of time for the TSX itself. The compound annual growth rate for the past 10 years is about 7.8% including dividends. Simple interest calculations would put the returns at 8 to 10%.

S&P

The Standard and Poor's 500 (S&P 500) is a common measure of the performance of the US stock markets. It includes about 500 of the largest US companies.

I looked back to 1979 providing a 35 year time horizon, which included many ups and downs in the market, including the major crash of 2007-2009.

Over that 35 year history, the S&P provided a compound annual growth rate of 8.79%. When you look at just the past ten years, which again included the most recent crash, the compound annual growth rate was 5.44% and simple averages were around 7%. Not counted in these numbers are the dividends that companies paid out to shareholders which was between 1% and 2% bringing the total returns for the past ten years to as high as 9%.

The Dow Jones Industrial Average which includes only thirty companies traded on the New York Stock Exchange shows similar results.

SPY

Just as you can't buy shares of TSX, you cannot buy shares in the S&P 500. But again you can buy an ETF that approximates the performance of the

S&P 500. One such ETF trades under the ticker symbol SPY.

SPY has a 21 year compound annual growth rate including dividends of 9.74%. Looking at the last ten years the compound annual growth rate including dividends has been 7.61%. Simple interest calculations come in at 8 to 10%.

DVY

Given that my strategy is a dividend growth strategy, and I believe that ETFs are a good form of investing, why not just find an ETF that follows the same strategy and buy that? Good question and not a bad strategy. There are several ETFs that attempt to do exactly what I do by investing only in strong companies that have a good track record of paying and increasing dividends. One such ETF is DVY. Here is the long term performance of DVY.

The earliest record I can find on DVY is late in November 2003 when it traded at $34.28 per share (adjusted for future splits and dividends), according to Yahoo Finance. Its actual trading value was about $50 at that time. At the end of 2014 it was trading at $79.40, which has already factored in any stock splits and dividends paid out. This assumes that you reinvested the dividends (about 3% per year) into the ETF.

Compound annual growth rate for this ETF is about 6 1/2 % for the ten years ended 2014 and slightly higher if you go back to 2003. Even a simple interest calculation shows a return of under 8%.

There is nothing wrong with using this simple approach to investing. However as you have seen, my returns for the past ten years have averaged about 10% including a dividend payout of close to 4%.

TD Bank

Here is an actual case history of a stock that I purchased and have held for over ten years. Toronto Dominion Bank of Canada is one of the big six Canadian banks. Canadian banks have proved to be the strongest in the world and not only weathered the stock market crash of 2007-09, but actually thrived. This is due to the fact the the Canadian government in the 1990s refused to deregulate the Canadian banking industry as was happening everywhere else in the world, especially in the US. Canadian banks cried and complained that they were unfairly being restricted in their activities, but in the long run this is what saved them.

You will see elsewhere in this book that I did invest in U.S. Bank, CitiBank, and lost almost the entire investment. Many US banks went through similar experiences. You may recall that during the crash the economy of Iceland collapsed due to the deregulation of the banking industry and subsequent risks that the banks imposed on the remainder of the country. Ireland suffered a similar fate. A joke going around at that time was: "What is the capitol (capital) of Iceland?" Answer: "$25".

Canadian bank shares dipped during the crash, but came back rather quickly and rose to record highs.

I purchased 200 shares of TD Bank in 2004 at a price of $46.30. It was paying a dividend of about 3 1/4% and had a history of increasing its dividend.

I now own 400 shares of TD bank, due to a 2014 two for one stock split and it is still paying about 3 1/4% in dividends on a share price of 55.51

(December 31, 2014). My initial investment of $9,316 is worth $22,200. Calculating simple interest that is over 13% per year, but recall simple interest inflates the return, so I prefer compound annual interest which calculates to be almost 8.8% per year. When you add the over 3% dividend per year the annual returns on this stock has been over 12%.

This is a true success story but the same has happened with all of the Canadian banks as well as many of the stocks I show on my suggested list and stocks that I own. However the most interesting feature of dividend growth stocks is the actual dividends themselves. On the surface it would appear that the dividends have not changed as the yield has remained constant at just over 3%. However companies do not issue dividends as a percentage of share price, they issue them as dollars per share. This amount per share increases each year, but if the price of the share increases as well, the calculated yield appears to remain the same. But the dividends calculated on your original cost continues to grow. My current yield on share price of 3 1/4% actually translates into over 8% on the original cost. If you were to buy a bond or term deposit at 3%, it would still be returning 3% on your cost. Dividend growth stocks show an increasing return on your original investment.

Coca Cola

Let's take a look at another of my early purchases of stocks that meet my long term criteria - Coca Cola (KO).

I purchased 200 shares in KO on September 23, 2004 for $40.07 per share at a total cost of about $8000. As a result of a two-for-one stock split, I now own 400 shares at a market price of $42.22 per share for a total value of $16,888 (December 31, 2014).

The compound annual growth rate is 7.52% since I purchased it and I have an annual dividend yield of 2.9% giving a total annual return of almost 10 1/2%. Simple interest excluding dividends is well over 10%.

Although the dividend yield on the market price is just under 3% the dividend yield on my original cost is over 6%.

Each of my early purchases of stocks within my criteria have a similar story, giving continuing credence to my strategy.

Not all of my purchases were as successful, but in retrospect, those failures would never have fit into my current strategy as a legitimate purchase.

Actual Stock Returns

Following is a list of stocks that I held for more than one year at the end of 2014 and their associated annualized returns excluding dividends. That is the average annual percentage gain in share price. The two worst performing stocks happen to be caught up in the current oil price squeeze and, being foreign oil companies, have been hurt by the strong US dollar, but are still paying a large and growing dividend.

Ticker	Average Annual Return
LMT	35.72%
NVS	21.10%
T.TO	18.43%
RY.TO	15.61%
TRI.TO	14.30%
ENB	13.87%
PM	12.83%
NA.TO	11.93%
INTC	11.63%
PWF.TO	11.58%
KO	10.66%
BCE.TO	10.21%
MRK	9.90%
KMB	9.57%
TD	9.40%
JNJ	9.27%
BMO.TO	9.24%
CM.TO	8.69%

FTS.TO	8.49%
PEP	8.46%
TRP.TO	8.23%
PG	7.89%
MCD	6.65%
DD	6.61%
MO	5.13%
UL	4.85%
COP	4.34%
GWO.TO	3.66%
T	2.79%
RDS-A	-1.52%
TOT	-14.29%

Chapter 11 - Financial Advisors

Should you use a financial advisor or not? In my early days of investing that wasn't even a question in my mind. In spite of being a professional accountant with an MBA, I always used a financial advisor. They are in the investment business and should know more than I do. It turns out that many of them actually have considerably more knowledge about investing than I do. However that knowledge seldom translates into superior results. But it can make for interesting intellectual discussions.

Most financial advisors do not have a provable track record of success with their own assets, so why take their advice? They mean well, but their income and livelihood is based on the type and frequency of your purchases and sales, not on how effective their advice is. I have yet to see the actual personal portfolio of a financial advisor nor have I seen evidence of their personal returns. They only talk about the returns they think you can get in the future.

Here are my experiences:

Lanny

My first experience with an advisor was in 1980 when I was approached by Lanny who was a mutual fund salesman for the Principle Group. I had a bit of cash from the sale of my parents' house and a small insurance claim from an auto accident. I bought some mutual funds that performed poorly and Principle Group went bankrupt. Fortunately their mutual funds were segregated and were not affected by the bankruptcy. However, poorly performing markets with poorly managed funds left me with a big loss. I really liked Lanny, but he really knew nothing and was just flogging his company products.

Charles

Almost everyone in Canada has been approached at some time by a mutual fund sales person from Investor's Group. In 1993 I needed a place to put my fully vested pension funds after leaving a long term employer. Charles, from Investor's, showed up at a most opportune time and my money ended up in his suggested mutual funds. The funds performed well but not as well as the general market which was hot during most of the 1990s.

I quite liked Charles as well, and we hit it off personally. This is a common theme with advisors. But he was far from an expert in investing. He was a typical Investor's Group salesman. He had been laid off from his management position while in his late fifties and had little in the way of employment opportunities. Therefore you go to Investor's Group and sell their proprietary funds.

I bought the funds that had no up-front fee, but had penalties for pulling your money out before a specified time period. The funds performed well as this was the nineties, but the performance was well below market. As I reached that time limit, which was around seven years, I pulled my money out and moved it to other investments.

In checking the Investor's Group Website:

http://www.investorsgroup.com/en/product s/invest/mutual-funds

you will see that there are expensive fees and very sub-par returns which are on public display for everyone to see.

Nice Old Ladies

I joined an employer who had an excellent RRSP program where they matched you dollar for dollar up to the legal limit of your contributions. I participated to the fullest as it increased my salary by almost 10% in doing so. The biggest downside was that all employees were required to use the company sponsored investment advisors who determined what investment options you could select from. This investment firm was owned and operated by a couple of older widows who knew absolutely nothing about investing or even the mutual funds they were promoting. They were very nice old ladies, but absolutely useless. I was not impressed with how my money was managed and found that I was not alone. All of the other employees felt the same. Time to change.

Todd

With the support of the other staff, I got permission from the company president to explore other options for investment managers. As controller of the company I was the natural choice to lead this initiative.

I went through a formal bid process to select a new firm, receiving proposals from several investment advisors and ended up selecting and advisor representing BMO Nesbitt Burns, the brokerage firm associated with the Bank of Montreal.

Todd turned out to be an excellent choice and was well received by all of the staff of our company. He did a good job at directing individual's investments to appropriate investments, most of which however, were mutual funds. As well intentioned as Todd was, he still needed to produce a personal income and the mutual funds provide the best compensation for investment advisors, which is why so many of them turn first to mutuals.

I stuck with Todd for several years as he moved from BMO to the investment arm of Toronto Dominion Bank and then to ScotiaMcleod, affiliated with the Bank of Nova Scotia, (ScotiaBank). I did begin to direct him away from mutual funds towards more direct stock investing, which became the beginnings of my current investment strategy. When Todd moved on to a management position within ScotiaMcleod, my portfolio was assigned to my current advisor.

As I began to accumulate some extra cash

outside of my RRSP, I maintained my own investments and began to develop my investment strategy and have done so ever since

David

As I mentioned earlier, I still use a financial advisor for my RRSP (similar to the US IRS). His long term returns are certainly satisfactory at around 7%. Being a registered fund he is restricted in what he can put in the fund. For example, we have decided jointly that 30% of my portfolio will be in fixed income instruments that do not perform as well in the current investment environment. Also he is restricted by regulation as to how much and what type of foreign investments can be in the fund. The Canadian market has not performed well in the past 10 to 15 years which has kept a lid on returns.

Originally my fees were based on the transactions I executed, using his advice. I then moved to an annual fee based on the size of my portfolio, which I felt would provide some incentive for growing my portfolio rather than just trading. It seems to have worked reasonably well.

That being said, he is still far behind what I can get trading on my own, but he still gets his fees regardless of the performance of my portfolio.

Conclusion

I would recommend that you don't use a financial advisor. If you do go with an advisor, use a full service broker who will follow your directions, not tell you what to invest in. The strategy suggested here is very low maintenance and requires very little effort or knowledge. You are only looking at a grand total of 40 to 50 stocks, not thousands. Most people will only own 10 to 20 stocks in their portfolio and will need to do very little trading. I hold around 40 stocks (which I consider to be too many and I am looking at reducing) and execute less than a dozen trades in a year, so the average person will likely only need to trade when they have new money and need to buy a stock, or on the rare occurrence that one of the stocks slips from grace and needs to be sold.

Chapter 12 - Real Estate

This section provides my commentary as well as references to many articles on housing in Canada and the U.S. I would encourage you to do your own objective research.

There are lots of reasons to buy a house as a place to live: lifestyle, family, hobbies, yard, etc. I even read one study that showed that children of home owners performed far better in school than those in families who don't own a home. I would never discourage someone from buying a house as their home as long as they can afford it. However I would discourage anyone from thinking that buying a home is an investment. There is a plethora of evidence to prove that a home is a money pit, rather than the route to riches.

A quick check of the definitions provided earlier will show that you would be hard pressed to consider your home an investment. If you want to invest in real estate for the purpose of renting - either commercial or residential - you will need to do your own cost benefit analysis. I am only reviewing real estate from the perspective of a home owner.

People seldom factor in the actual cost of owning a home such as routine maintenance, insurance, taxes, major repairs, renovations and the costs associated with purchasing and selling a home.

When people think of the return on houses the normal calculation they make is the selling price compared to the purchase price. They seldom include all of the ancillary costs associated with home ownership and the purchase and selling transactions, such as legal fees, land transfer taxes, and real estate commissions. So when you see data on increases in house prices, they never factor in the other costs.

According to TD Bank, the long term (1980 to 2012) return on real estate in Canada was 5.4% per year (2.4% when adjusted for inflation). This nominal return is before considering any of the extra costs of home ownership. Compare this to the return on the Toronto Stock Exchange in excess of 9% (over a similar time frame) with none of the additional costs.

You can always come up with anecdotes of a relative or friend that made a fortune on real estate just by buying and selling homes. These aren't fabricated stories, they are true accounts. By the same token you can find similar anecdotes of those who made a fortune with lottery tickets. The key to investing is whether you can enter into an investment and obtain predicable and sustainable results. Those lottery winners and home price winners would be hard pressed to repeat their performances and there are more losers than winners.

I have one friend who insists that you never lose money on real estate. He has at various times owned up to three properties in the UK, one in Abu Dhabi and one in Turkey (on which he lost money twice). He has lost considerable money on each property but still insists this is the safest place to put your money, because you never lose on real estate. Sometimes facts don't matter.

General Real Estate Information

We are bombarded regularly with news reports of escalating house prices. This creates a panic situation with many people making you feel like you had better jump in or you will miss the band wagon. I know I felt this way, resulting in my rushing to get into the housing market and continually upgrading my premises so I too could have the biggest and best house I could afford. I began with a starter home in 1972, moved up to a larger family home five years later and then ten years after that, I moved to a luxury home. I don't regret my home ownership years, but now that I'm older and wiser and use more facts than emotion in my financial decisions, I see how I could have been financially more secure today, perhaps even retiring a couple of years earlier, had I made different housing decisions. In retrospect I see that my home choices were more about lifestyle than investing, and that's OK. I now drive a new Altima, rather than a more economical Sentra. However, I could easily afford an upscale Infinity. It's a lifestyle choice and as long as you can afford the lifestyle you want, there is nothing wrong with those choices. I don't consider my automobile purchases as investments, and home ownership is no different.

Generic Data

Following are randomly gathered data on the real estate market in Canada and the US, just to provide some perspective on housing as an investment. If you are looking at housing as investment, scan these articles and do your own research and run your own numbers. However, if you are looking at real estate as a home, all you really need to consider is whether or not you can afford it.

—-

Calgary House Prices history (from a 2010 article)
http://calgaryrealestatereview.com/2010/07/29/calgary-historical-average-house-prices-sales-timeline/

Excerpt:

During the early 1980's boom/bust, Calgary average house prices peaked at $110,184 (Total MLS) in January 1982. Prices bottomed out in November 1984 at $68,322 – at 37.99% drop.

The next peak was in July 2007 at $442,693 (remember, that's using old criteria) with the next low in January 2009 at $363,706 – a 17.8% decline. Last month, the average price was $417,875 which is down 5.6% from the peak.

These statistics are based on average prices. But what is an average house? If there are more houses sold at the high end that will artificially inflate the number and vice versa.

Here is a quote from an article on house sizes.

> http://www.outsidethebeltway.com/size_of_average_american_house_doubled_since_1950s/

Excerpt:

The average American house size has more than doubled since the 1950s; it now stands at 2,349 square feet. Whether it's a McMansion in a wealthy neighborhood, or a bigger, cheaper house in the exurbs, the move toward ever large homes has been accelerating for years.

Consider: Back in the 1950s and '60s, people thought it was normal for a family to have one bathroom, or for two or three growing boys to share a bedroom.

***

Here is another look at house sizes:

> http://answers.google.com/answers/threadview?id=110928

Excerpt:

According to the US Census, new built homes in the United States increase in square footage between 400 and 500 sq ft every 20 years. In 1950, the average square footage of a single family home was 1,000 square feet. In 1960, the average square footage of a single family home was 1,200 square feet. In 1970, the average square footage of a single family home was 1,500 square feet. In 1980, the average square footage of a single family home was 1,595 square feet. In 1990, the average square footage of a single family home was 1,905 square feet. In 2000, the average square footage of a single family home was 2,265 square feet. In 2001, the average square footage of a single family home was 2,330 square feet.

***

And one more:

http://www.theglobeandmail.com/globe-investor/personal-finance/mortgages/our-love-affair-with-home-ownership-might-be-doomed/article4179012/

Excerpt:

In 1975, the average size of a house in Canada was 1,050 square feet. Fast forward to 2010 and new homes being built almost doubled to an average of 1,950 square feet. This increase in house size is accompanied by a decrease in the average number of people living in a household. In 1971, it was 3.5; by 2006, that number fell by a full person to 2.5.

***

More on housing as an investment – from the Wall Street Journal:

Don't Buy a Home as an Investment

http://www.wsj.com/articles/dont-buy-a-home-as-an-investment-1419728902

Excerpt:

3.7% average annual growth over 30 years not counting carrying costs (insurance, maintenance, fees, taxes, etc.)

(Note by author: I'm getting more than that on dividends alone and there are no carrying costs.)

Here is some advice for young people who are thinking of "investing" in property:

"The average national house price rose about 5.8 per cent annually on average over the past 30 years, which is a great result from an asset that is supposed to merely keep up with inflation. But the Canadian stock market averaged 9 per cent annually over that period with dividends included." (Globe and Mail, May 25, 2015)

The 5.8 per cent increase in housing prices does not include taxes, fees and maintenance which would drop that number to under 4%.

More data

Some quotes:

http://homeguides.sfgate.com/average-rate-return-real-estate-investments-72195.html

Single Family Residences

The returns on single family residences are relatively low. Based on the well-respected Case-Schiller index of home values, the average home has gone up in value just one percent per year after inflation over the period from 1890 through 2005. Since many rental homes in and around expensive cities like San Francisco offer minimal or, in some cases, negative, cash flow, the returns on holding them are relatively low.

Here is a quote from a Forbes article in 2005 on real estate vs stocks:

But if you take a longer view–say 25 years–you'll find that the S&P 500 has actually stomped the real estate market, from Boston to Detroit to Dallas. From the start of 1980 to the end of 2004, home sale prices increased 247%. A pretty sweet deal, it would seem. Over the same period, however, the S&P 500 shot up more than 1,000%.

Real Real Estate Examples

Enough of the general market, now for some first-hand analysis.

These are scenarios that actually happened, not hypothetical "would have, should have, could have" made up situations.

My Childhood Home

My first experience with home ownership was when I was too young to even know there was a difference between renting and owning a home. In 1962, my parents bought their first home under the Diefenbaker home ownership program allowing them to purchase a house they otherwise could not afford. The price was $12,000.

We had to move seven years later when my dad was transferred to another city. He was able to sell the house for $18,000. It was a shame to have to move, as my dad and I had put in a lot of effort to upgrade the bare bones new home. We started with a dirt yard and nothing around it. We built a fence, installed a lush lawn and lots of garden space, not to mention a bunch of trees that were just beginning to produce shade when we had to move. During the seven years in the house we did some interior upgrades as well, including converting our wall-to-wall broadloom to hardwood floors.

A simple calculation would show an annual return on this investment of over 7% per year. But that is before selling fees, maintenance and upgrades, and city property taxes. The compound annual growth rate upon the 1969 sale was actually under 6% and by the time you factor in the other costs the return was under 4%.

But what if we had kept that house until today? I have driven by the house several times over the years when visiting that city. After all, those seven years formed my growth from child to adult. I have watched it change from the outside - new fence, garage, repainted several times, and who knows what else has been done to the inside.

It now sells for over $400,000 - a far cry from the $12,000 paid for it 52 years ago; quite the return. But again if you do the math, the compound annual growth rate on this investment is under 7% less any maintenance, upgrades and taxes. Once you deduct the actual additional costs of owning this home, your annual returns would likely not exceed 4%.

And now to our next house:

My parents purchased a house in the new city for $18,000 in 1969. It turns out it was an even swap for the house it replaced, except for the transaction fees on both ends. That same house now sells for $248,000 or an increase of almost 1,300% over 45 years or 28% per year. But again if you apply the principles of compound interest, which is what you do when investing, the annual return is under 6% after considering selling fees. Taking maintenance and taxes into consideration, this ends up being under 4% per year.

What about being a landlord - isn't that better?

When my parents died, this house became mine, along with the existing mortgage, maintenance costs and property taxes. Checking the rental rates I found that my cash inflows would exceed my cash outflows, which any property investor will tell you is all that matters in real estate investing. I've already proved that any equity would be better served in the stock market than in property, so the claims of increasing your net worth with growth of housing prices doesn't hold water.

I chose to rent out the home to provide additional income.

My first tenants were a doctor from India, his British wife and their young son. They were great tenants who became our friends. If all tenants were like them I might still be a landlord. They were low maintenance and very easy to deal with. But they eventually wanted their own house and moved on.

The second tenants were an older couple who used to be resident managers for an apartment complex. I guess they knew the ropes when it came to tenants' rights. They were a nice and respectful couple, but very demanding as tenants. I was not sad to see them move out. Although they didn't cost me too much money for all of their demands, I seemed to be constantly on call for them, totally disrupting the rest of my life.

The third tenants were a couple of Chinese

university students that morphed into what appeared to be the entire population of China in my rental house. Every room, complete with tenant suppled locks, was filled with roommates and the driveway was filled with Trans Ams or the poor man's equivalent - the Chevy Vega.

This was a low maintenance crowd and left the place completely intact when they finished their school year and moved on. In spite of the appearance of chaos, it ended up working out OK.

During this five year period, my bank account never seemed to improve, in fact it deteriorated. The house barely paid its way on a month to month basis once the mortgage, taxes, insurance and associated expenses were counted. The market value of the house appreciated, but not by much. I was tired of being a landlord and put the house up for sale.

As many people have learned, the market value of a house seldom bares any resemblance to what you actually get when you sell. By the time you accept an offer and pay the fees, you don't have nearly as much to deal with as you had expected. A house is not a liquid asset and just because you put it up for sale, don't expect the cash to arrive quickly. It sat empty on the market for several months with no action. I even resorted to putting it back on the rental market to at least generate some cash flow. Fortunately, I finally got an offer I could accept - but not love. It was far less than what was in my mind when I mentally calculated the value of the house.

I pocketed less than $30,000 after paying off the mortgage, taxes and fees. This plus around $3,000 dollars on an insurance settlement from a car crash that destroyed my dad's VW Rabbit, represented the entire inheritance from my late parents. The $30,000 in 1985 in fact represented the total gains from the $12,000 house originally purchased in Calgary in 1962.

But I now had some cash in my possession - something I had never really experienced since I purchased my first house. I could now be an investor. I took most of the cash and put it into RRSPs (IRA for American investors), catching up on some of my previously unused capacity, and kept out $10,000 for my next poor investment detailed elsewhere in this book.

Summary - $12,000 house purchased in 1962 resulted in $30,000 cash in 1985. Depending on how you calculate the values, that amounts to a 4% to 6% compound annual growth rate, not counting all the expenses incurred in operating a home for almost 25 years - taxes, insurance, maintenance, upgrades, etc.

My brief encounter as a landlord should not necessarily serve as an example of what owning property and renting it out is like for everyone. If you want to purchase property for producing revenue, that is entrepreneurship - owning your own business. I am not devoting any time in this book to running a business - only in investments.

My First Home

I purchased my first home in 1972, shortly after I married. We were fortunate in that the federal government had just initiated a short-lived low-income house purchase plan. I was earning $325 per month as a clerk in a pipe mill and my wife was earning $300 as a teller in a bank. In those days banks considered 100% of the husband's salary and 50% of the wife's salary when determining mortgage eligibility. Using this formula, we did not qualify for low income housing - our combined salaries were too low. We were below the level of low-income families.

I was able to convince my employer to fudge my numbers and factor in some expected salary increases and we were able to just cross the line into the realm of low-income Canadians, thus being able to qualify for a mortgage. The government chipped in the down payment, giving us a mortgage of about $16,000 at 7 5/8 percent annual interest resulting in payments of $128 per month, which included principle, interest and taxes. Incidentally, those not qualifying for the low income housing program had to pay several thousand more for the same home.

I was very fortunate to get into this house at that price. Many of our friends paid thousands more for the same type house less than a year later.

We were now home owners and joined the ranks of those possessing a money pit. We were always amazed at how much of our free cash was gobbled up in just keeping the house going. Being a low-income house, it didn't come with any frills, such as screen doors or closet doors, or even a dryer vent. The latter was not a big deal because we couldn't afford a washer and dryer and relied on a washer spin dryer.

However, all of those little extras had to be dealt with over time. We had to haul in proper loam to allow for grass to grow. We built a fence around our over-sized lot. I put in a concrete driveway and finished the basement with a rumpus room and a study for me to use in upgrading my education so we would eventually not be "low income" anymore.

After five years of pouring money into our tiny low income house we found that it no longer accommodated our growing family which now included two young boys and we traded up to a larger home and started the whole process again.

I often wondered what would have happened if we had kept that house? What would my financial situation be like now? I have checked on the current value of the house and it comes in at $224,500. Using simple math, that amounts to a whopping gain of 1,300 percent in the 42 years since I first purchased it. Again, simple math tells you that that is over 30% per year. That is a terrific investment - how can you not win on owning property with returns like that.

Not so fast - simple math is for simple minds and results in not so wealthy home owners. The compound annual growth rate on that investment is just under 6 1/2 percent. That means that if you invested $16,000 at 6 1/2 percent per year and left it growing for 42 years you would have $224,500. Six and a half percent, although lower than what you would get in the stock market, still sounds pretty good doesn't it? But that doesn't consider the fact that you would have to pay transaction fees of at least 5% upon sale, reducing that return. Also remember the "money pit" mentioned above. I doubt that the new owners of that house got away without continually putting cash into the upkeep of their home. For example, I doubt that our shag rug from 1972 still graces the floors of the living room, hallway, and two bedrooms. Most estimates put annual maintenance costs at about 1% of the current value. At that rate, the annual return is now down to just over 5% per year. In addition the annual property taxes in that city are just under 1% of the current property value, bringing the annual return to around 4%.

Now compare that return to comparable returns in the stock market and you are at less than half. That doesn't mean that you shouldn't buy a house to live in, but don't be too quick to pat yourself on the back over your shrewd investment. Things aren't always as they appear. You may say that at least you didn't throw your money away on rent, however if you look at the section below on rent vs buy, you will see that argument doesn't hold water either.

My second home

We were able to get into our second house, a considerable step up from our first house, five years later. We didn't even have to sell our old house as the builder agreed to take it on trade as our down payment. As a result of that transaction it is really difficult to determine how much we got for our old house and how much we actually paid for our new one.

Our second house required all the same care as our first house - fence, yard, driveway, basement, plus a garage. Other maintenance included replacing water heater, furnace etc. It is easy to come up with the 1% annual maintenance fee, and I also saw the almost 1% every year going to the city for our property taxes (other cities may have lower rates).

I had this house assessed at $72,000 in 1986 when we decided to rent it out as we moved to another city where I would obtain my master's degree, allowing me to earn more income to pour into home ownership.

That house now sells for $274,000 showing a 280% increase over 28 years which gives you a simple return of 10% per year. Sounds comparable to my stock market returns, doesn't it? Not when you consider that the compound annual interest rate is actually under 5%. Again you need to adjust for selling costs, maintenance and taxes resulting in under 3% per year. You can do better than that with a term deposit - even in today's low interest rates.

A New City

I was fortunate to get a paid leave of absence to obtain my MBA from 1986 to 1988. With some financial assistance from my employer I was actually able to purchase a home in the city where I went to university so my family would have a stable environment while I studied.

I purchased the house in 1986 for $88,000 and sold it two years later for $105,000. Sounds like an easy quick buck with almost a 20% gain in two years giving almost 10% per year in returns. However there was a 7% real estate fee upon sale making my gross take only $97,650. I was frugal and did not put in any maintenance into the house knowing that we would be out in two years, but I did have insurance and taxes.

When you calculate compound annual interest and factor in the insurance and taxes, my annual return was actually under 5%. This was during a time when real estate prices, especially in that city, were exploding.

The Lap of Luxury

I purchased my last house, my luxury home, in 1989 for $105,000 - another money pit. I sold this house in 1993 for $109,000, barely making enough "profit" to cover the real estate fees. During this period of time the average house prices in that city grew from $71,000 to $73,000 so I guess I beat the market, with a barely calculable annual return.

After finally doing some analysis on the real cost of home ownership, I decided to get out of home ownership altogether. It was good over the years to have a place for my children to call home and a yard to play in, so it wasn't a waste. But now my children were grown and no longer needed the security of our home - and I wanted to do other things with my life.

I moved into rental property and have had excess cash ever since.

One More Example

I could go on endlessly with real examples of real estate returns, however I will stop with one more.

A good friend just sold his family home after living in it for over 40 years. It is in a premiere district in a major city that has always been a hotbed for real estate in Canada.

He originally purchased the property for $27,000 in 1972. He sold it in 2015 for $517,000. How can you possibly beat a return such as that? But again doing the math, the compound annual growth rate is close to 7% but this house has undergone many major renovations over the years making the average annual maintenance cost of 1% seem rather small. Also when you compute city taxes and the selling cost of the house the real return is just over 5%.

This was their family home where they raised their children and had a great lifestyle, so I would never say that this was a bad choice. However as an investment it does not come close to what you will get with other investments. Also keep in mind this is one family living in the same house for over 40 years. Most people will actually move several times over that many years, increasing the cost of ownership and reducing the actual returns.

Summary

I never actually lost money on any of the homes that I owned. This is in stark contrast to many people I know who did in fact lose money on home ownership. However, as an investment, you see that the returns are dismal in comparison to the alternative of the stock market - especially when you measure over long periods of time. Real estate can provide you with a nice home, but it is not an investment.

Rent vs Buy

You need to live somewhere, so why not purchase anyway? Why throw your money away on rent? That is the common mantra from those who just want to own property and are not prepared to look at the actual numbers. You will find that renting, rather than owning, will actually increase your net worth, while owning your own home may in fact reduce your net worth, or at least reduce your ability to increase your net worth.

Here is a real example of rent vs buy situation. This is the condo in which I currently live. I have enough cash that I could easily buy the unit rather than rent as I currently do. Why throw your money away on rent when you can have equity in a home? The current owners would be elated if I would buy it and take it off their hands.

Below are the actual numbers for my current home. I pay $2,400 rent on a condo that would cost me $410,000 to purchase. Actually given the current market conditions the owners have dropped the rent to encourage us to stay. I can choose to buy and not pay rent, but then there are many other costs associated with owning that you don't have when renting - maintenance, taxes, condo fees etc. Also when you sell a home there are a variety of fees and costs that consume some of the money from your sale. All of the numbers below are conservative, in that they are favourable to the purchase option. For example, I did not factor in all the costs you incur when you purchase a home, such as legal fees, inspection costs and in some jurisdictions, land transfer fees. You could justifiably alter those numbers to something that favours renting more, but I have tried to not skew the analysis. You can try it yourself on a spreadsheet and adjust the numbers as you see fit. I have chosen the time period from December 2013 to December 2025 or twelve years. I am making the assumption that by that time I will be ready to sell and move into a retirement home. Renting comes out ahead over this period by more than $40,000 or over 8%. Using longer time frames only increases the difference.

maintenance	0.50%	$2,050.00
Property Tax	0.50%	2,050.00
condo fees	1.00%	4,100.00
inflation rate	2.50%	
rate of return	7.50%	
House Price Increase	5.00%	
selling fees	5.00%	
Purchase Price	$410,000.00	
Monthly Rent	$2,400.00	

If I were to purchase this condo for $410,000 and housing prices increased by 5% per year (remember compounding), I could sell the property after twelve years for $701,000. Sounds pretty good doesn't it? That's a 71% increase. However, I would not get $701,000. I would get $701,000 less any real estate fees and closing costs. I have conservatively used 5%, but selling could easily cost you more than that. This leaves you with not $701,000 but rather $666,000 or a 62% increase instead of the 71% we thought we were getting.

Then there are the annual costs. During the time I owned it I would have paid out over $130,000 in various costs of ownership. Taking that into consideration I would only net about $535,000 on my sale or about 30% on my original cost - less than half of the 71% I thought I was getting. You could easily justify using higher costs, but again I am trying to keep it conservative and unbiased.

So that's the case for buying. Now what if I choose to rent instead. My rental cost is currently $2,400 per month and I have assumed that it will increase by inflation each year. Again that is a generous assumption as my rent is actually going down. As a result, over the same period of time I will have spent over $397,000 on rent. Some would argue that this is just money thrown away. But remember, I have enough money to buy this home, so what do I do with that money? I invest it. For this example I have used 7.5% return on investment, but you will see that also is a conservative number as I have a long term return of 10%. My $410,000 will have grown to over $976,000. When I deduct the $397,000 of rental costs over that time, I am left with $579,000 which is $44,000 more than under the option of buying.

Why do I rent rather than buy? The simple reason is that it is cheaper and thus better for my net worth. Renting is not the same as throwing your money away.

I have done this exercise on many other properties and come up with the same result. At best purchasing will match renting, but it is never financially better. Run your own analysis, but be sure to include all the costs and use realistic assumptions. You will find that most people who try to do this analysis, purposely or by accidental omission, skew the numbers to favour purchasing. Don't be fooled with faulty math.

Chapter 13 - Market History

Here is an historical overview of major events in the markets in recent years.

Black Monday - 1987

The largest stock market crash since the Great Depression occurred on Monday, October 19, 1987. Markets around the world dropped anywhere between 20% and 60% in a single day, the DJIA dropping 22%. Experts still don't agree on the causes but regulations and procedures were put in place to avoid the panic selling that made matters worse.

The markets were fully recovered within two years and those adopting a conservative investment strategy had nothing to worry about in the long run.

The Fabulous Nineties

Any fool could make money investing in the nineties and many did. Many of the blowhards that serve as analysts and experts today, made their reputation and their money in the nineties. None of them have made a useful prediction since - just watch any of the financial shows on the major networks and/or on the financial networks. They make predictions and recommendations that are almost always wrong.

The prime example was Jim Cramer who told the NBC audience that they should sell all of their stocks at the bottom of the 2007-09 market crisis.

This was the most stupid advice ever given. Those that followed his advice locked in their losses and never recovered. Those who didn't listen to him (and I count myself among them) did just fine.

Back to the nineties - it didn't seem to matter what you invested in, it did well. The dot com bubble mentioned later was a prime example.

I did quite well with my lackluster mutual funds. I saw them go up (never comparing my returns to the market returns) so I thought I was pretty smart. There were years when my portfolio growth exceeded my earnings. It felt good.

There will be times like this, called a bull market, when everyone prospers. You can't participate if you're not in the market. The market goes up and the market goes down. You can't predict (no one can) when the ups and downs will occur, so you just have to be there to enjoy the good times; which means you must endure the bad times as well.

Specialty and speculative investing

During the frenzy of investing in the 1990s one segment of the market soared - precious metals, especially gold.

Everyone had gold fever and were pouring money into mining stocks, particularly a Canadian company called Bre-X.

Bre-X was a penny stock with an investment in potential gold properties in Borneo. Published reports on the samples taken from this mine indicated that this might be the biggest gold deposit ever found on earth. Everyone, and I mean everyone, wanted a piece of this action. The stock price soared as "intelligent" investors, including institutional investors sunk every penny they could find into this company. At the peak the market capitalization of Bre-X was $6 billion. It accounted for a significant part of the unprecedented growth of the precious metals index and by extension, the TSE (now the TSX).

By the peak, Bre-X had not actually extracted a single ounce of gold from this rich deposit and had not turned a single dollar of revenue. The value of the company was based entirely on investor exuberance.

If something is too good to be true, it probably isn't true. This was the case with Bre-X. This play was one of the biggest frauds in the history of mining - and that's saying a lot. There was no gold deposit, the stock became worthless, every investor lost all their money invested and the TSE dropped accordingly.

Another reason to stick with proven strong revenue producers with a history of dividends.

Dot Com Bubble

This was a great example of the herd mentality that investors can fall into. As with housing, investors are afraid to miss the next big thing - the next bandwagon that you can't afford to lose out on. In the 90s, technology was the big thing. The Internet was in its infancy and everyone wanted to jump on. Thousands of start-up companies with great ideas began developing their software solutions to carry their potential customers into the twenty-first century. To raise money for their ventures, these start-ups flocked to the market of the future - the NASDAQ. The index for this market rose from a number well below 500 in the early 1990s to over 5,000 during the year 2000. Everyone wanted a piece of the action and there was no end in sight as to how high the technology index would go.

Most of the companies driving up the index had little to no revenues, let alone any profits. You couldn't even measure the PE ratio because there was no "E". The hype was based entirely on what everyone thought the future would hold in the way of riches for these intelligent investors. Then the bottom fell out for the imaginary companies and most just vanished along with the hard earned money of the greedy hoards. Many of these folks expected to retire early with their new found riches. I met one couple in the Middle East, when I moved there, who had just come out of an early retirement based on their imaginary riches. They had lost everything and had to return to work for a living.

The NASDAQ index fell below 1,300 and has never reached the same heights as during the bubble.

Established companies with proven sales, profits and dividends, were not affected by this turmoil. They continued to thrive and grow and spin off dividends as they had done for years. Anytime someone says "This time is different - times have changed," just nod politely and walk away. Stick with what works.

The Lost Decade

This is the term that is used to describe the stock market from 2000 to 2010. The market indexes were almost exactly the same at the end of the ten year period as they were at the beginning indicating no growth and no returns. This ten year period also saw the big crash of 2007-09.

If you were invested in dividend growth stocks you would have at least seen a return from your dividends. The dividend growth stocks did quite well during this period of doldrums in the market.

I actually ended the ten year period with a significant growth in my investments, many of which are discussed on other pages here.

Global Financial Crisis - 2007 to 2009

During this period the economy of the entire world collapsed - stock markets, real estate, entire industries, entire countries (e.g. Iceland). I was living near Dubai which at that time was one of the hottest markets in the world for real estate, capital and employment. I watched as Dubai went from a bustling city to a shell of its former self with dozens of unfinished buildings and thousands of cars abandoned at the airport as ex-pats fled in fear of being held accountable for their local debt obligations.

I won't get into the causes of the crisis as I am

not an expert and there are thousands of others who have written about what propagated what is called the worst financial crisis since the Great Depression. However high-risk banking practices, hedge funds and an overheated real estate market (especially in the U.S.) played a major role.

The Dow Jones Industrial Average went from a high of over 14,000 in October of 2007 to a low of just over 7,000 in February 2007 - a 50% drop. A drop like that requires a 100% gain to get back to where you started. Some people, especially those in mutual funds, saw their portfolios drop as much as 80%.

I was fortunate enough to be sitting on a large stash of cash at this time while waiting for some buying opportunities. (See my discussion on individual stocks). As a result, my portfolio dropped by just under 15% from its peak in late 2007 to its low point in February 2009. By the fall of 2009, I was fully recovered and on the way to new heights. The Dow Jones didn't fully recover until early 2013.

This again speaks to the wisdom of sticking with a solid and proven strategy.

Chapter 14 - Flubs and Prizes

As my strategy evolved, I made several purchases and sales that seemed to fit with my changing criteria. Some were good calls, or maybe a bit lucky while others were dismal failures and never should have been considered for my portfolio. Fortunately my good luck trumped my bad calls before I landed on the "right" strategy, while still ahead of the game. Here are some of the more notable examples.

Flubs

Here are some examples of my more notable failures. Most of these losses came as a result of me relying on advice of others rather than sticking with a tried and true strategy. These types of mistakes would not occur under my current strategy, with the exception of BP which found itself in a tough situation.

General Electric - GE

In the 2004 to 2006 time frame, I used the Dogs of the Dow strategy to start and grow my position in another Dow 30 high-yield company. GE had been around forever and would never disappear - right? Well it didn't disappear, but 50% of the company was into financial activities that took the biggest hit during the financial crisis. GE survived, but its financial arm did not. My $12,000 investment had shrunk to just over $7,000 when I disposed of it in 2012.

BP

I purchased $12,000 of shares in BP on April 23, 2010. It fit perfectly with my now established strategy. ValueLine A++, High dividend yield and a long history of giving and growing dividends. Then the unimaginable happened. What seemed like a relatively unconnected event occurred on April 20 with an oil rig disaster in the Gulf of Mexico. Although not a BP activity directly, it was quickly linked to BP and all hell broke loose. By the first week in May I realized that my nearly 20% loss was not going to recover quickly and I sold, licking my wounds. Normally I would just stay the course and ride it out, but this looked outside of normal, especially when BP was forced politically, not financially, to suspend its annual dividend. The market is very unforgiving of such actions and the stock plummeted. My early action prevented further losses as the effect on BP was devastating and long-lasting.

Allied Irish Bank - AIB

Watching the success of high dividend yield bank stocks around the world, I purchased about $12,000 worth of shares in AIB in the spring of 2007. As the market crash unfolded, I watched this stock dwindle away to the point it was no longer considered worthy of being listed on any stock exchange. High-risk banking activity claimed another victim and my $12,000 was history.

ANHEUSER BUSCH - BUD

One of my losers during this phase of dividend stocks was BUD. Also purchased for its dividend capacity in 2004 for about $10,200, I sold it in 2006 for just under $8,600. This loss had nothing to do with market conditions, it was just a bad choice.

CitiBank - C

I bought this stock as part of the Dogs of the Dow strategy in the fall of 2004. How could you go wrong with a high dividend yielding company that was a member of the prestigious Dow Jones 30? After all even the Abu Dhabi Investment Authority, reputedly the largest sovereign investment company in the world, took a significant stake in this enormous world-wide bank. My $9,000 investment would surely return me riches.

The market crash of 2007-09 proved how fragile even the largest of corporations can be. Years of deregulation allowed US banks to embark on high risk activities unchecked. This is really the root of the market crash, and the value of the shares fell to nearly zero, putting CitiBank in a position to nearly go bankrupt, as many other financial institutions did.

With a bit of manipulation, a bit of a government push, stiffing the existing shareholders, and with a reverse stock split, the company survived looking like nothing had ever gone wrong.

I sold my shares for around $500 virtually wiping out my initial investment. I was able to absorb my loss with my other more intelligent investments, but I have often wondered what happened to the trader who bet the farm in Abu Dhabi on this classic tale of loss.

Wells Fargo - WFC

In 2004, using a modified Dogs of the Dow strategy, I purchased about $12,000 of this high-yielding US bank. It took the same hit as the remainder of the US banks during the stock market crash, but having not engaged to the same extent in high-risk behaviour, it recovered from the crash and I sold with a 9% loss in early 2010, after the recovery.

***

<u>Prizes</u>

Here are a few examples of some of my better moves, but I can't necessarily claim anything more than a bit of luck. Some were very lucrative, while others were average at best.

Nortel

During the 1990's while working with Todd, my financial advisor at the time, I purchased a position in Nortel, one of Canada's biggest telecommunications related companies at the time. At one point Nortel accounted for about 30% of the value of the TSX (TSE at the time). This was one hot stock that seemed to keep reaching for the stars. I watched my money triple in a short period of time while the company issued two back-to-back 2-for-1 stock splits while the value of the shares kept climbing. No one was prepared to guess how high this stock would go, but there seemed to be no end in sight. In talking to Todd I asked him how high it would go and he said, "Who knows?" I told him that I wasn't greedy, why not just take the profits and if I lose out on further growth, so what. So he sold my position and looked for other opportunities for the cash.

Only days later, shares in Nortel started to drop and kept dropping. It dropped well below my original cost and eventually fell to a penny stock and the company filed for bankruptcy leaving shareholders with nothing.

The lesson I learned from this was not to be afraid to take your profits and run. I did this several times after that experience.

Imperial Tobacco - ITYBY

In March 2006 I bought Imperial Tobacco (an ADR on the NYSE) - 160 shares at just under $60 for about $9,600. This is a British company traded on the NYSE that fit my criteria at that time of a high and growing dividend. A year later the stock had jumped to over $91 giving me well over a 50% gain plus a healthy cash dividend. Given that this was more of a gain than I could ever have expected from dividends, I sold the stock and sat on the cash to await further buying opportunities.

E.On - EONGY

This is a European utility company that traded on the NYSE as an ADR. It again fit with my criteria in 2006 of high and growing dividends. I purchased 300 shares at just under $43 and in a year the stock had skyrocketed to almost $56 and I sold, to sit on the cash awaiting buying opportunities, having pocketed a 30% gain plus cash dividends.

SPY - S&P ETF

In 2004 I started dabbling in ETFs with a fund that mirrors the S&P 500. As mentioned earlier, the 10 years ended 2010 saw almost no growth in the general market and I sold my position in SPY in 2007 with a modest gain of 7% - again providing cash to sit on as the financial crisis unfolded.

SDY - dividend ETF

While experimenting with Exchange Traded Funds (ETF), I purchased SDY which is a fund that invests only in strong dividend producing companies, this fitting my criteria at the time. I acquired just under $9,800 worth in 2006 and then sold a year later when I decided to move to direct stock investing rather than ETFs. I made about a 15% gain plus dividends. Another bit of cash that sat out the crash.

RSP - dividend growth ETF

This was another ETF I purchased in 2004 which invested in dividend producing companies. I bought about $22,000 in shares which I sold in 2006 for just over $24,000 giving me about a 10% gain plus dividends.

General Mills - GIS

In 2004 as part of my dividend strategy, I acquired about $10,000 of GIS. I sold this position in 2007 with about a 10% gain plus annual dividends.

Disney - DIS

Another dividend play in 2004 was DIS. I purchased it in 2004 for $9,600 and sold less than 2 years later for $11,400 - an 18% gain plus dividends.

Vectren - VVC

In 2007 I ventured into a utility company because of its stable and growing dividend. This was just before the crash. I paid $11,000 and sold at a break even in 2010, just after the recovery from the crash, after watching the stock plummet along with the rest of the market.

Canadian National Railway - CNR

I purchased $11,000 worth of CNR shares in 2005 and sold it for almost double in 2011 when I was looking for stocks with higher yields. Although this was the right move for my objective of providing a dividend stream, CNR continued to grow and would have been a good hold.

Power Corporation POW

I bought and sold POW in the 2005 to 2007 time frame, holding it for about 26 months. This was while I was still experimenting with my dividend strategy and of course before the market fell apart. I made about a 22% return over this short time frame while receiving an annual dividend yield of about 3 1/2%. Note that POW is very closely aligned with GWO and PWF, being part of the same overall corporation.

Great West Life - GWO

I purchased 300 shares at 29.31 of GWO in March of 2006. This was while I had a dividend yield strategy and I was mainly looking for yield. Financial stocks were especially vulnerable to the crash of 2007-09 and GWO took a big hit, leaving me in a loss position. By the time the crash was ending, I had almost fully developed my current strategy and found that GWO still fit with my strategy, so I not only held on, but added to my position buying 400 more shares at a price of 22.27 in October 2012 while I was still in a loss position with my current holdings. As of December 2014 the share price sat at 33.59 leaving me with a $4.28 gain or nearly a 13 % profit. That is only a return of less than 2% per year, but a pretty good recovery for a stock that tanked during the market crash. During this time of volatility I still received my cash dividend of over 3 1/2 %, making it an acceptable return, especially considering the effects of the crash. Of course my 2012 purchase has soared with a 50 % growth in 14 months plus the healthy dividend. This is a good example of holding on to good stocks even when the going gets rough.

Toromont Industries - TIH

I held this stock for about a year from 2006 to 2007, again while experimenting with dividend stocks. The TIH yield is just over 2%.

My gain was just under 8% for the year plus the dividend and I sold it in favour of looking for higher yielding stocks.

Chapter 15 - My History

Here is some background on my history with managing my money. This may give you some insight on how I got to where I am now - complete with some bonehead moves. There are lessons in this that I learned, but this section is more for entertainment than lessons.

Childhood

When I was very young, my father had a dispute with his long term employer and left in a snit. With little marketable skills (in 1954) he resorted to being a stock broker. It has always been easy to get into these kind of sales positions, but not as easy to make a living. We almost starved and my dad went back to his previous employer - hat in hand and got his old position back. We always lived hand to mouth although I always felt we were well off, as I never had to do without. However my dad was always in debt, unbeknown to me. By the time he retired, my dad had paid off all his debts except for the house mortgage, and when he died three years later, his net worth amounted to the small equity in his home, a few thousand dollars and an older model Volkswagen Rabbit.

I learned nothing about investing from my dad - he never invested a penny and saved little. However he did teach me something about saving. When I was old enough to understand about money, I started receiving a weekly allowance. Supposedly it was for doing my assigned chores, but being my dad's only child, I was assigned very little. The original allowance was around 50 cents per week and with raises it peaked out at $2 per week. My dad took me to the bank to open a bank account and insisted that I place at least half of my allowance in the bank. I asked him when I should start withdrawing my money and he said, "Never". "What about if I need to buy something?" I inquired. "If you need to buy something, then use the money that wasn't put in the bank." I guess he was trying to teach me a lesson that he wished he had employed.

By the time I was nineteen and in university, I had amassed about $600 in my savings account. In need of a car to use for my first real job one summer, by father "allowed" me to withdraw $300 to purchase a used 1963 Plymouth Valiant with a slant six engine and a three-on-the-tree manual shift.

I was now grown up and working and my bank account was getting larger. I spent most of my first summer's wages on an engagement ring and matching wedding bands for the woman of my dreams. The rings outlived the dream. The dream lasted for 25 years, but the rings have lasted much longer. My youngest son and his wife are now wearing the rings I purchased with my summer earnings. That "investment" has lasted well over 40 years.

Koscot

I never got burned by the pyramid schemes that have circulating since eternity. As pyramid schemes have been made illegal in most jurisdictions due to many "investors" being taken in prior to the mid nineteen-seventies. These schemes are now called multi-level marketing programs, there are still many of them around and you will always find people at the top making lots of money, while those at the bottom slave away to provide their masters with big incomes and lots of perks. The current versions comply with law and as such are not illegal, but perhaps bordering on unethical.

That said, I did get tangled up with the Koscot crowd of the early 1970s at nineteen years old. Thanks to the wisdom of my father, I never did "invest" any money - mainly because I didn't have any money and my father refused to finance my venture.

But that didn't stop me from being enthralled by the spellbinding narratives of its founder, Glen Turner and his many devoted followers.

Koscot was probably the original successful pyramid scheme, and was the impetus for legislation banning the existence of pyramid schemes, forcing their replacements to structure as multi-level marketing schemes.

Koscot initially sold cosmetics that were produced from mink oil. The concept sounded fine as a product, but to Glen Turner and his followers, the real riches came from selling distributorships, not the product. Although there was an actual product, it was seldom mentioned. You made your money by getting a commission from convincing others to invest in the company and then they would go out and do the same. As in a chain letter, the early participants can do quite well, but further down the pyramid is a chain of broke participants.

Koscot began to fall apart when they moved from a tangible product to selling a concept or idea of self-improvement. Koscot begat "Dare To Be Great", which was just selling "rah rah" seminars, a couple of manuals and some cassette tapes. Then came the end of pyramid schemes as we knew them at the time.

Over a several month period I watched as many common folk invested thousands of dollars into this get-rich-quick scheme and lost everything in the long run. But I also witnessed many of them grow and mature as they went through the process of learning how to recite their pitch.

One of the pitch lines that always stuck with me was that 95% (according to them) of all people would live in poverty or near poverty by the time they reached retirement. The pitch was "Do you want to be part of that 95% or part of the 5% who enjoy their golden years?" I was determined to be part of the 5% and that guided many of my future decisions and actions, many of which, as you will see, were less than successful.

Based on the information Koscot provided, I was sold on the quality of the product.

***

Here is a story I wrote for my future memoirs on my experience with Koscot.

Koscot
Regina – 1971

"In order to understand Koscot, you need to understand Epcot – Experimental Prototype Community of Tomorrow." This is how every presentation started out. Koscot stood for Cosmetics (stylized with a 'K') for the communities of tomorrow. The room was filled with 20 to 30 people. All but about five of the audience was already invested in Koscot. The five "outsiders" were prospects for "distributorships". A $5,000 investment would allow them to sell directorships and dealerships to other people in exchange of a share of the take. Oh, and incidentally, there were some cosmetics involved as well – but only incidentally.

What attracted me to Koscot was the product itself. However, not many people really wanted to talk about the product. The base for most cosmetics was lanolin, or as Koscot people called it "sheep sweat". Koscot cosmetics had as its base, mink oil. US patent reports hailed mink oil as the closest animal substance to human fluids.

I attended many of these "rah-rah" sessions. Lots of cheering, clapping and pounding of fists on doors and walls. The idea was to get people excited about being rich. "Did you know that 95% of the people retire poor? Do you want to be one of them, or one of the

5% who end up rich."

I didn't have $5,000, and I was sure that my dad didn't have $5,000 for me. Alan and Larry Bogdan had invested the $5,000 from their farm income and planned to be rich. I was their prospect. But I was less ambitious. I saw real opportunity for the product rather than selling distributorships. So I was looking at the possibility of buying in at the $1,000 level as a "supervisor."

I talked Dad into coming with me to one of the sales sessions. I was pumped, but Dad had been around the block a few times and saw it for what it was worth – a scam. I asked Dad for the $1,000, but he turned me down flat. One of the few times Dad ever said no to me. And he was angry when he said it – another unusual feature for my dad. I pondered my next move.

In the meantime, Alan and Larry still saw me as their best prospect. Glen W. Turner, founder of Koscot, was travelling to Winnipeg to give a motivational session to his "flock" and any prospects they could attract. Alan and Larry invited me to come with them.

I was treated to one of the glitziest mass presentations I have seen in my life – even to this day. Mr. Turner came out dressed in a mink coat and had a couple of twin dwarfs, also dressed in mink coats. They bragged about all the money they had made and encouraged the thousand or so people in the hall to join them in the elite club of millionaires.

When I couldn't get the money to buy in, I got dad to spring for $29.95 to buy a sales kit. This gave me the demo product I needed to sell the product to ladies. I attended training sessions to learn about the product and its application. I tried for months and made precious few sales. Then I started to realize what my dad was getting at. If the product couldn't be sold, then what value is the distributorship. I wish I had have remembered that lesson ten years later when I fell into a similar trap.

Anyway, after not succeeding as a cosmetic salesman, I turned to vacuum cleaners. Rainbow, here I come.

Rainbow

With Koscot out of my system now, I was determined to make a quick buck somehow, so I was very susceptible to any scheme that reared its head.

A couple of my university buddies convinced me to look at a place they were now working at which supposedly provided a large ($460 per month) guaranteed income for just demonstrating an air purification system in people's homes. How could you lose? This would be more income than I could hope to get upon graduation, so I gave it a try.

It turns out the guaranteed salary was only guaranteed if you sold enough of the Rainbow vacuum cleaners. They didn't like to use the term vacuum cleaner, but that is what it was. I gave dozens of pre-arranged demonstrations in people's homes without receiving a single dollar of the guaranteed salary. I finally made one sale after dozens of rejections, but that sale was returned within the four day limit provided by law. So after two months of being a vacuum cleaner salesman, I left poorer than when I started.

Joe and Harold, the owners of the Rainbow franchise, also owned the franchise for Lifeware Cookware pots and pans. They tried to recruit me to sell this line of business to young ladies thinking of getting married and starting a home. But I was finished with door-to-door sales.

AB Dick

My brother was branch manager for AB Dick in Winnipeg and later in Saskatoon. AB Dick was an old, established, privately owned office equipment company that had decided to go public. My brother mentioned this to me and said that he was going to buy a bunch of shares because it was a great company and he could make lots of money on the shares.

I barely had two sticks to rub together having a monthly salary of less than $400 per month but I thought I needed to get in on this sure thing. I was able to scrounge together about $500 and located a brokerage firm that could transact my trade. I had never bought shares before and didn't have a clue how to go about it. The brokerage firm didn't seem too interested in seeing this twenty something kid with $500 in his hand but finally assigned me to one of their tired old brokers who looked like his next move would be out the door or out the window.

He was quite patient with my total ignorance and tried to guide me through the process of share purchases. First of all the commission was about 7% of the total purchase price, so I would be investing my $500 less the 7% that he would share with his company.

The next thing he explained to me was that shares were normally traded in 100 board lots, which meant that you bought 100 shares or 200 shares or 1000 shares or 1100 shares. This was the days before computer trading and splitting a lot was a difficult task. Given the price of the newly offered shares of AB Dick, my cash would only buy me 15 shares. I think he would rather I just drift away, but I persisted and he said he would try to put in a buy order for 15 shares.

After a few days he called me back to say that my order had been placed and I was now the owner of 15 shares of AB Dick. Now all I had to do was watch my money grow. But how was I to watch it? The only public source of stock market information was the daily newspaper and it contained a reasonably thorough list of stocks traded on the Canadian exchanges but only a selected list of stocks on the New York Stock Exchange, where my shares were apparently trading. So the only way I could get a stock quote was to call my broker on the phone and ask him to look it up for me. I did this almost daily during the first few weeks, and again my broker patiently looked up my stock and gave me the quote. I would do a quick calculation and determine how much I had made. My $500 grew (in spite of the commission paid) to $550, then $600 and above. My calls decreased to weekly and then monthly as the growth seemed to abate and my investment seemed to plateau at around $650. I resorted to infrequent calls as I was getting tired of looking at the same number each time and it was several months before I made another call. I had probably held the stock for well over a year by this time. When I did my calculations I found that I was now at about $300. I made the broker repeat the quote several times before it sank in that I had actually lost some money.

I called up my brother to see what was happening, after all, as branch manager for AB Dick he should know. He told me he wasn't following the share price at all and that he had sold his shares a long time ago after making a bundle. He advised that I should probably sell my shares too.

By the time I was actually able to get my broker to find a buyer for my 15 shares I was able to pocket about $200 - a loss of 60% on my first ever investment. It would be another ten years before I ventured back into the investment arena.

Principle Group

In the early 1980's I had a bit of extra cash from both an insurance claim when my dad's old VW Rabbit was totaled in an accident I had and the cash from the sale of my parent's house. With an eye to investing, I was susceptible to listening when sales people called with an investment idea.

I received a phone call from Lanny (see earlier comment on financial advisors) who was a salesman with Principal Group of companies. I liked his approach and allowed him to make a pitch for his investment proposals. Principal Group, out of Edmonton, was started by an entrepreneur and had become quite a conglomerate in western Canada. It had a trust company (operating very similar to a bank) and a set of proprietary mutual funds.

Being an accountant I felt I could fully understand the details of what was being pitched to me. Although I had heard of mutual funds for many years, actually going back to my youth, I had never bought any. These funds had a front load fee - that is a commission to purchase the units, but with the excellent guidance of the fund managers, this commission would be insignificant. Right?

My state of readiness to purchase some kind of investment vehicle superseded my otherwise logical and skeptical nature and I purchased several thousand dollars of a variety of funds and put them in an RRSP for tax sheltering purposes.

The early 80's saw a major recession in Canada and my investments soon began to shrink in value. On top of that, the excellently managed Principal Group ran into difficulties and went into bankruptcy, causing thousands of people to lose money on their deposits. Much of that was recovered through the mandatory deposit insurance that financial institutions had to carry, but that took years and was subject to limits.

Fortunately for me, I was in segregated funds that were kept separate from the actual company and were secured by the stocks held within. Unfortunately, the markets were at a very low point and my value was considerably less than I started with.

I arranged to have the remaining funds transferred to a deferred annuity with the insurance company with which I was employed. It would be a while before I ever considered investing again.

This, my second venture, into the stock market was another dismal failure.

Toy Business

With a bit of extra cash and the desire to diversify my investments, I allocated 10,000 of the funds from the sale of my parent's home to invest in a business. I wasn't intentionally seeking out a business venture, but I spotted an opportunity in a newspaper ad and decided to follow up on it.

The ad was very brief, but indicated you could be a distributor of high end children's toys. With our children at an age where toys were important, this looked like a perfect fit. It would also allow for productive use of my wife's time as she was still a stay at home mom, but with lesser commitments now that the boys were in full time school.

I made contact the company and met Gary in his hotel room for a discussion of the opportunity. He made his pitch and being good with numbers I felt his conservative estimates were quite realistic and this could be profitable - not get-rich-quick profitable, but slow and steady income generation.

For the cost of your investment of $10,000, the company would supply you with 15 fully stocked displays which they would install in several retail establishments on a consignment basis. This would include locations such as grocery stores, gift shops, kiosks etc. After the 15 company supplied locations, we would be free to increase locations as we saw fit. Our job would be to restock the displays and manage the consignment arrangement with the retailer.

Given the margins, which seemed reasonable and conservative sales numbers of $15 dollars per day per location, this investment would payback in about a year and then we would be into profits. It was hard to see how you could lose. Especially given that they would give you $10,000 worth of product to begin with. I ran the numbers over and over and couldn't see any problems.

Under the usual pressure of "act now or lose your opportunity", I transferred the $10,000 and awaited the delivery of my product. This was a tense time, because if the product didn't arrive, I would have subscribed to a well-executed scam. I had done my checking as best you could in the pre-internet days by going to the Chamber of Commerce and Better Business Bureau and all seemed to be legit.

But no worry, my product arrived not long after and the delivery company put a bunch of boxes of brand new toys and well-constructed display stands into our basement. Now we just had to await the arrival of the company installer who would select and set up our initial 15 locations. We were excited.

Within 24 hours of delivery of my goods, I received a phone call from the truck driver who delivered my goods. It turns out that he too had invested in this toy company and also had 15 display stands and a $10,000 inventory of toys. Being the delivery company of choice he told me that he was aware of another dozen people who had done the same. Everyone had their product and display stands but the originating company was now out of communication.

I, as all of the others, thought that I had exclusive rights to the local market, but that was not the case. There was definitely not enough room in the market for all of us.

We formed an informal group and met regularly to discuss our options. Several of the other distributors had been in contact with the company which now seemed to be going out of business, meaning our source of supply would be gone. It wasn't a full-fledged scam in that they did deliver the product that they promised, but did not supply the retail establishments as promised and would not be able to deal with resupply. The resupply was not much of an issue, as amongst us, we had enough product to supply the local market for a couple of years.

We all decided that we would try to set up our own retail locations and resupply from our stock, to at least minimize the losses. Eventually this loosely aligned group disbursed and didn't amount to much. My wife and I decided to find our own outlets and discovered that this was quite a chore. Franchise outlets, like the airport store, were controlled by their head office and would not consider local consignors. We did find about four places where we could set up on consignment, but the daily sales were far less than the $15 we thought we would get. Eventually all the locations asked us to pull our displays.

With the sales from the locations, private sales and using many of the toys as gifts for birthday parties, that we would otherwise be buying, and tax write-offs, I was able to keep my net loss to only a couple thousand dollars, making this a relatively inexpensive lesson.

Chapter 16 - Now to Today

None of my "investment" ventures provided any returns. Most of them actually sucked my reserves dry. So what then? I turned to the tried and true method of becoming a millionaire - I saved what I could of what I had.

Where my money came from:

Income - I started work in late November 1971 as a clerk in a pipe mill at a wage of $325 per month. I continued to study accounting, becoming a professional accountant. My salary increased each year to the point where my salary just before retirement in 2014 was about $100,000 per year - 43 years of working for a salary. I had some good years of income where my salary was above $100,000, but until the last few years of employment, I seldom had sustained income above $75,000 per year.

Inheritance - when my parents died in 1980, I inherited a 1976 Volkswagen Rabbit which was later involved in a total loss accident providing me with a $4,000 insurance settlement. I also inherited my parents' house along with its mortgage. I rented it out for a couple of years (see analysis under "Real Estate") and then sold it. My net cash, after using some of the cash for failed investments, was about $25,000.

Severance package - in 1993 I was laid off from a long term employer and received about $75,000 in severance. I used that money to live on while I spent the next several months securing alternate employment, but was able to put a significant amount into savings.

During my employment years, I raised two sons (with the constant help of a stay-at-home mom), put them through a dozen years each of competitive hockey, then four years each of university, and then went through a divorce after twenty-five years of marriage, splitting our net worth at the time equally between the two of us.

So as you can see, my current net worth comes from saving from my earnings and using a sound investment strategy along with a disciplined execution to put my savings to work for me.

Summary and Conclusion

I am not rich, but I am financially comfortable in retirement. I have accumulated my net worth by saving money from my earnings and investing it wisely and conservatively. I invest in safe secure stocks of large dividend producing companies. There is nothing magic or complicated about how I approach investing and anyone with a bit of cash and some interest in controlling their financial future can do what I am doing. I have made my share of mistakes before finally settling on my current successful financial path. If you can avoid similar early mistakes, your financial future could be even more secure than mine.

I hope that this book has provided you with some useful information and perhaps even a tidbit of entertainment. I am more than willing to talk to anyone who has further questions, but I am not interested in making money off other people's savings.

For my benefit, but also for the benefit of future readers of this book, it would be great if you could post a review on Amazon or Goodreads or even better, both places.

Thanks for taking the time to read.

Brian Borgford

brianborgford@hotmail.com

https://borgfordinvesting.wordpress.com/

Now that you have embarked on Financial Fitness, why not start on Physical Fitness. Follow my other journey to health and fitness in my book:

From Couch Potato to Weekend Athlete

Available at Amazon.com where you can read my other books.

http://www.amazon.com/Brian-Borgford/e/B0088L0ULC

Made in the USA
Columbia, SC
28 November 2017